SKILLSTUFF

The basic skills activity encyclopedia for teachers

Volume II. Writing

by KIDS' STUFF Authors
Imogene Forte
Joy MacKenzie

Library of Congress Catalog Card Number 79-91211
ISBN Number: 0-913916-80-3

Printed in Nashville, Tennessee
United States of America

by

Williams Printing Company

WHAT'S IN SKILLSTUFF WRITING?

The Skillstuff Check List sequentially grouped
in basic skills areas
- . . . Using Words and Phrases
- . . . Using Technical Writing Skills
- . . . Composition and Original Writing
- . . . Writing for Everyday Living

Model Activities—one or more for each skill

Teacher Lesson Plans—specific skills objectives, preparation and student directions.

Student Worksheets—ready for reproduction and use

Competency Reviews—informal mini achievement tests for each of the four skill areas.

And Lots More—teacher yellow pages offering lists and lists of rules for capitalization and punctuation, proofreader's marks, puns, writers' aids, etc.

HOW TO USE SKILLSTUFF WRITING.

To Teach Basic Writing Skills:
Use the skills check list to find out where kids are and what they need to do (you'll find blank ones ready for reproduction on the back of each section title page).

Select and use activities to meet individual or group needs (the indexed skills check list following the Table of Contents will speed up this step).

Use the competency review to determine if and to what extent the skill has been mastered.

Begin planning for the next cycle and start over!

THAT'S WHAT SKILLSTUFF WRITING IS ALL ABOUT.

—just a quick and easy approach to diagnostic/prescriptive instruction in basic writing skills.

> . . . and to add flair and excitement unique to your own teaching style, use all yellow page goodies to design more and better games, worksheets, and individual and group tests and projects.

ACKNOWLEDGEMENTS

Special acknowledgement is gratefully accorded

...to Mary Hamilton, who illustrated the book, and to Gayle Seaburg Harvey, whose artistic flair contributed to the cover and the section title pages,

...and to Elaine Raphael, editor par excellence.

TABLE OF CONTENTS

WRITING FOR EVERYDAY LIVING

SKILLSTUFF: WRITING CHECKLIST

Student's Name	Grade	Date	Teacher's Name

I. USING WORDS AND PHRASES	SKILLSTUFF Activities

PARTS OF SPEECH

____ Nouns   17

____ Verbs   18

____ Adjectives   20

____ Adverbs   21

____ Words Used as More Than One Part of
Speech   19, 22, 23, 24, 25

WORD USAGE

____ Synonyms, Antonyms, Homonyms   26, 27, 28

____ Multiple Meanings   29, 30

____ Comparisons   31, 32

____ Plurals and Possessives   33, 34, 35

____ Preciseness   36, 37

____ Abbreviations and Contractions   38, 39, 40

____ Avoiding Clichés   41, 42

VOCABULARY DEVELOPMENT

____ Internalizing Word Meanings   43, 44, 45, 46

____ Finding Alternatives for Overworked Words   47, 48, 49

____ Using Jargon and Current Vocabulary   50

II. USING TECHNICAL WRITING SKILLS   SKILLSTUFF Activities

USING PUNCTUATION MARKS   55, 56, 57, 58

____ End Punctuation

____ Commas

____ Apostrophes

____ Quotation Marks

____ Colons and Semicolons

____ Parentheses

USING CAPITAL LETTERS   59, 60, 61, 62, 63

SPELLING   64, 65, 66, 67, 68

WRITING SENTENCES   69, 70, 71, 72, 73
                                                         74, 75, 76, 77, 78,
____ Four Kinds of Sentences   79, 80, 81, 82, 83,
                                                         84, 85
____ Writing a Good Sentence

____ Fragments, Complete Sentences

____ Run-On Sentences

____ Subject-Verb Agreement

____ Sentence Structure

____ Parallel Construction

WRITING PARAGRAPHS   86, 87, 88

____ Writing Topic Sentences

____ Organizing a Paragraph

IMPLEMENTING MULTIPLE WRITING   89, 90, 91, 92, 93,
SKILLS   94, 95, 96, 97, 98,
                                                         99, 100, 101

III. COMPOSITION AND ORIGINAL WRITING   SKILLSTUFF Activities

COLLECTING AND ORGANIZING IDEAS

____ Using a Variety of Resources   106, 107, 108
____ Sequencing Thoughts   109, 110
____ Note Taking, Summarizing   111
____ Paraphrasing   112, 113
____ Précis Writing   114

USING FIGURATIVE LANGUAGE

____ Metaphors and Similes   115
____ Personification, Alliteration, Onomatopoeia   116, 117, 118, 119, 120

USING SPECIAL LITERARY DEVICES

____ Sensory Appeal   121, 122
____ Point of View   123
____ Puns   124
____ Emotional Appeal   125, 126
____ Unusual Perspective   127
____ Imagery, Mood, Parody, Irony, Hyperbole   128, 129, 130

USING PROSE FORMS

____ Characterization   131
____ Description   132, 133
____ Dialogue   134
____ Narrative   135, 136
____ News Reporting, Editorials   137, 138

USING POETIC FORMS

____ Rhymed (couplets, rhyme schemes, etc.)   139, 140, 141, 142, 143
____ Unrhymed (haiku, cinquain, quatrain, free
        verse, etc.)   144, 145, 146, 147, 148,
                                            149, 150

WRITING TITLES, CAPTIONS, AND LABELS   151, 152

EDITING AND PROOFREADING   153, 154, 155, 156

IV. **WRITING FOR EVERYDAY LIVING**	SKILLSTUFF Activities

LETTER WRITING

_____ Friendly, Social Notes, Business	161, 162, 163, 164
_____ Envelopes	165

INFORMATIONAL AND INSTRUCTIONAL WRITING

_____ Graphs and Diagrams	166, 167, 168, 169
_____ Signs and Posters	170, 171, 172, 173
_____ Pictorial Directions	174
_____ Procedural Directions	175
_____ Geographical Directions	176, 177, 178, 179

COMPLETING INFORMATIONAL FORMS

_____ Identification and Registration	180, 181, 184
_____ Applications	182, 183
_____ Contracts	185
_____ Order Blanks	186, 187

ORGANIZING AND RECORDING FACTUAL DATA

_____ Record Keeping and Inventories	188, 189, 190
_____ Memos	191
_____ Biographies	192, 193
_____ Bibliographies	194, 195
_____ Checks and Deposits	196, 197
_____ Journals and Diaries	198, 199, 200, 201
_____ Lists	202, 203, 204
_____ Ads	205
_____ Reports	206

SKILLSTUFF

Using Words & Phrases

SKILLSTUFF: WRITING CHECKLIST

Student's Name	Grade	Date	Teacher's Name

I. USING WORDS AND PHRASES	SKILLSTUFF Activities

PARTS OF SPEECH

____ Nouns

____ Verbs

____ Adjectives

____ Adverbs

____ Words Used as More Than One Part of Speech

WORD USAGE

____ Synonyms, Antonyms, Homonyms

____ Multiple Meanings

____ Comparisons

____ Plurals and Possessives

____ Preciseness

____ Abbreviations and Contractions

____ Avoiding Clichés

VOCABULARY DEVELOPMENT

____ Internalizing Word Meanings

____ Finding Alternatives for Overworked Words

____ Using Jargon and Current Vocabulary

THE NAME GAME—NOUNS

Everybody knows that a noun is a name of a person, a place, or a thing.

Don't forget, some nouns name things you can neither see, touch, smell, taste, or hear—such as prayer, democracy, greed, and friendship.

If you tried to make a book of all the nouns you could think of, you'd very quickly run out of paper and patience! So let's narrow the focus to one subject you are especially interested in right now, and see how many nouns you can write related to that subject in just ten minutes. (Please try for some unusual ones!)

VERB ADVENTURE

Use old magazines and newspapers to help you in your "Verb Adventure." Look for three or more verbs that show some action that would be possible for each of the nouns in the pictures below. Cut out the verbs you find, and paste them beside the correct pictures.

NAME A NERB

Color in all the spaces in which a word appears that can be used both as a noun and as a verb.

If your answers are all correct, your pattern will reveal a very important person!

ADJECTIVES AT WORK!
HANDLE WITH CARE

Adjectives are used by writers to help the reader see a person, place, or thing as they see it. They are sometimes overused and misused simply because the writer thinks that "more means better."

Rewrite the following sentences using fewer adjectives to make a clearer, more interesting sentence.

1. She ate the shiny, rosy, red apple. _____

_____

2. A gigantic, ferocious animal was glowering hungrily over their shoulders.

_____

_____

3. My mother's new dress is absolutely, divinely, beautifully lovely.

_____

_____

4. Yesterday's sunset was a splendidly vivid, multicolored burst of rainbow hues. _____

_____

5. Fury, the large, black, long-legged stallion, galloped onto the track in splendid triumph.

_____

_____

6. I tried your grandmother's special, old-fashioned, butter and egg recipe for butter brown cookies.

_____

_____

STAR WARS

Do battle with yourself—Star Wars style! In one galaxy, each star must be supplied with a three-syllable adjective. In the opposing galaxy, each star must be supplied with a three-syllable adverb.

Do one galaxy at a time, and time yourself to see which galaxy wins the battle!

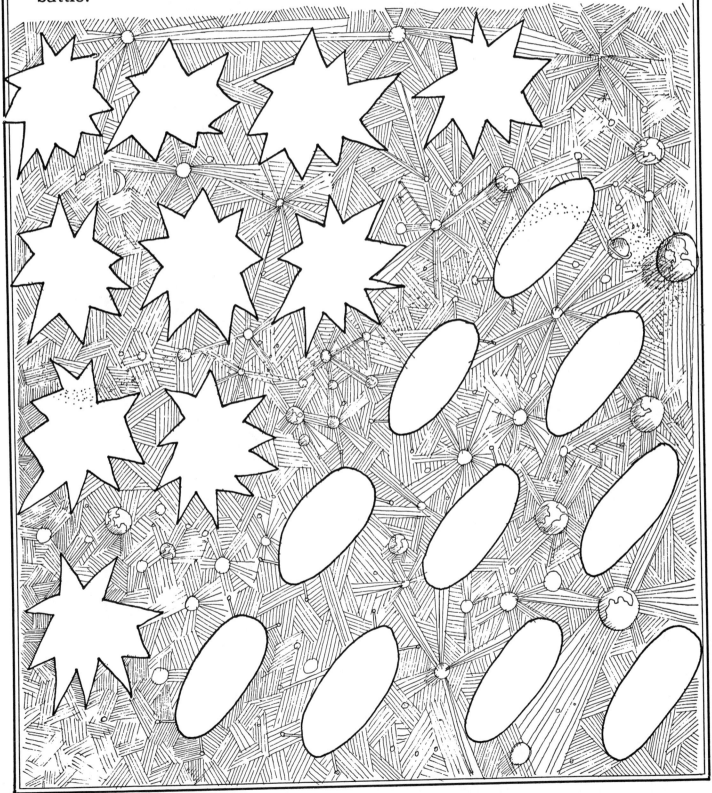

ARE YOU A WORD WHIZ?

Take this Word Whiz Quiz to find out if you are a real Word Whiz.

Tell what part of speech each word in the sentences below is by writing the proper number from the Word Whiz Code in the space under each word.

1. Oh! You frightened me!

— — — —

2. Please don't do that just now.

— — — — — —

3. Ethel and Henry are good friends.

— — — — — —

4. Will the mail arrive soon?

— — — — —

5. Pumpkin pie is a favorite of mine.

— — — — — — —

6. Are those tigers dangerous?

— — — —

7. Those children are skating on thin ice.

— — — — — — —

8. Help! This house is on fire!

— — — — — —

9. The weather is improving slowly.

— — — — —

CODE

NOUN	1
VERB	2
ADJECTIVE	3
ADVERB	4
PREPOSITION	5
CONJUNCTION	6
PRONOUN	7
INTERJECTION	8

WORD WHIZ

PURPOSE: Using nouns, verbs, adjectives, and adverbs

PREPARATION
1. Write the following ten sentences (or make up your own) in large letters on a piece of heavy paper or tagboard.

    1) The striped flag hung limply from the pole.
    2) The silly saucer slid sideways across the lawn.
    3) A gorgeous girl kissed the befuddled major gingerly.
    4) Mischievously, the elves crept under the rug.
    5) Go quickly! The grumpy baron waits impatiently.
    6) Nine apes chorused their discontent loudly.
    7) The stingy miser meted out his money begrudgingly.
    8) Croaking crickets lept lazily from bush to bush.
    9) Haughty ladies often lose face.
    10) The sun beamed benevolently upon the drenched travelers.

2. Place the paper or tag in a protective acrylic sleeve, or cover it with clear contact paper.

3. Reproduce a copy of the following activity page for each participating student.

4. Place these items and some well-sharpened pencils, along with the procedure directions, at a specified activity center.

PROCEDURE
1. Read each of these 10 sentences carefully to identify all nouns, verbs, adjectives, and adverbs.

2. "File" each noun, verb, adjective, or adverb by writing it in the proper "file drawer" on your activity page.

3. Then rewrite each sentence, supplying new nouns, verbs, adjectives, and adverbs of your own choosing in the space provided at the bottom of your activity page.

1. _____
2. _____
3. _____
4. _____
5. _____
6. _____
7. _____
8. _____
9. _____
10. _____

BOXED IN

Write a *noun* to name the object in each box.
Write an *adjective* that could be used to describe it.
Write a *verb* that tells what it might do.

HIDDEN HOMONYMS

Find a hidden homonym in this word find puzzle for each boxed word in the sentences below. Write the word in the space beside the sentence. Then, using that word and the name of the person in the sentence, write a new sentence.

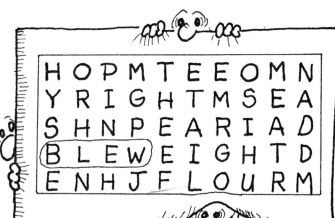

```
H O P M T E E O M N
Y R I G H T M S E A
S H N P E A R I A D
B L E W E I G H T D
E N H J F L O U R M
```

Example: Maria loved her new [blue] dress. __BLEW__

__MARIA BLEW BEAUTIFUL SOAP BUBBLES.__

1. Thomas told a tall [tale] . _____

   _____

2. Mr. Turner's [flower] garden is in full bloom. _____

   _____

3. Iced [tea] is Benjy's favorite drink. _____

   _____

4. Connie has a new fountain [pen] . _____

   _____

5. Jenni likes to [write] letters. _____

   _____

6. Fred will [meet] me at the pool. _____

   _____

7. This is Jim's last [pair] of socks. _____

   _____

8. Can Anna [wait] a little longer? _____

   _____

9. Rita wanted to [see] the show. _____

   _____

26

FRIEND OR FOE

In the word list below, find a pair of synonyms for each pair of friends and a pair of antonyms for each pair of foes. Write them in the spaces provided by each picture. (Hint: You may have some words left over!)

hate	mistake	love	full
cry	fat	end	foolish
come	weep	day	thin
wet	finish	arrive	night
error	silly	safe	dry

OPPOSITES ATTRACT

An antonym is a word that means the opposite of a given word.
Draw a line from each of the words in column 1 to its pictured antonym in column 2.

COLD

FEEBLE

HUGE

WELL

HURL

MEET

NEAT

ALL

SCREAM

ACCEPT

BOTTOM

STRAIGHT

GRAFFITI CHAMPION

PURPOSE: Using multiple word meanings

PREPARATION
1. Create a niche or corner with wall or bulletin board space for the graffiti suggested in the illustration below. Add a desk or table at which two or more students may work at a given time.

PROCEDURE

1. Introduce students to the free choice interest center, read the wall graffiti, and discuss the many meanings of the word "order." Let them suggest examples of additional meanings.

2. Write the following words on a chart or chalkboard, and add others that you or the students contribute.

run	turn	take
link	trunk	up
back	order	set

3. Direct each student to select one of the words to use in writing a creative story or poem. Develop, reproduce, and distribute a worksheet on which each student lists as many meanings as possible for the word chosen before beginning the writing project. Students should then make every attempt to use each meaning of the word at least once in the project.

4. When all stories have been completed, place students in groups according to their chosen words. In these small group settings, each student reads his/her story or poem aloud to the group. Papers may then be collected and placed in one folder to be added to the reading center, or they may be displayed on bulletin boards.

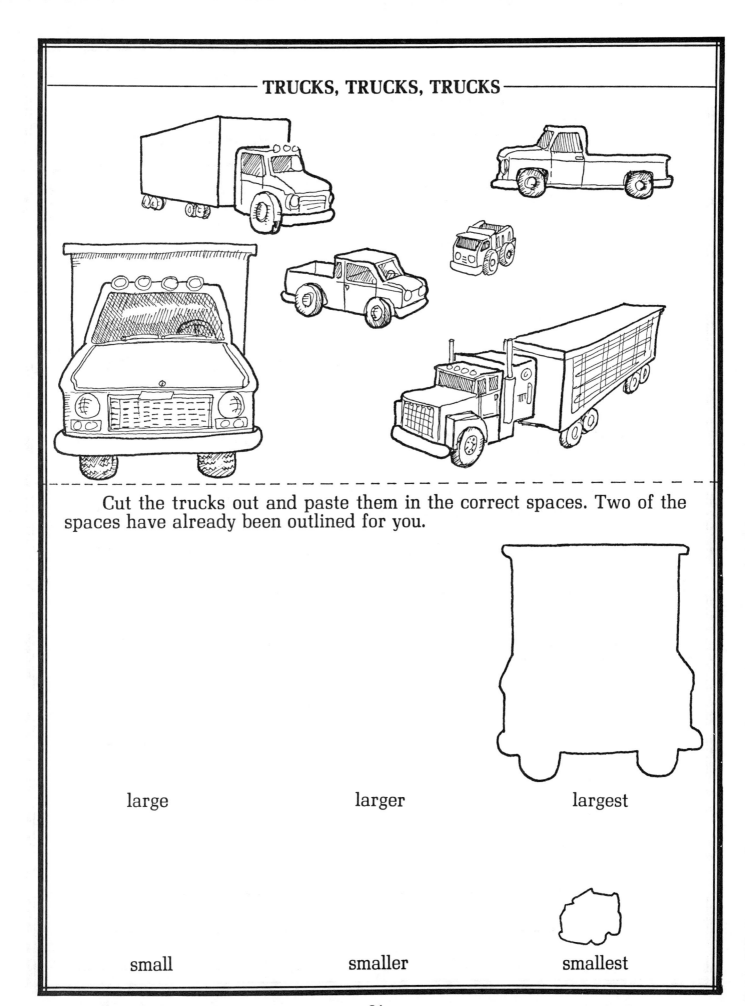

Cut the trucks out and paste them in the correct spaces. Two of the spaces have already been outlined for you.

large   larger   largest

small   smaller   smallest

From this list of comparative words, select three other comparison groups that could be used to describe the trucks.

small	smaller	smallest
narrow	narrower	narrowest
thin	thinner	thinnest
wide	wider	widest
funny	funnier	funniest
long	longer	longest
short	shorter	shortest
fat	fatter	fattest

Write them here.

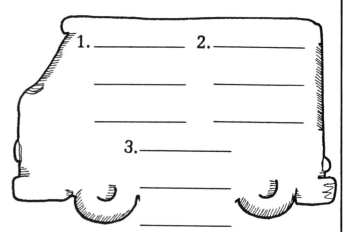

1. _____   2. _____

_____   _____

_____   _____

3. _____

_____

_____

If you think three of the trucks are beautiful and you want to compare them that way, you would have to say that
one truck is *beautiful,*
one truck is *more beautiful,*
and one truck is *most beautiful.*

How would you compare them if you wanted to use the word *elegant*?

elegant _____   _____

Write a paragraph about the trucks. Try to use at least three different comparative word groups.

_____

_____

_____

_____

_____

_____

_____

_____

THESE LITTLE PLURALS WENT TO MARKET

Help Mr. Dubbich make a sign for his market. Print the names of ten items for sale on the sign. Be sure to add **-s** or **-es** as needed to show more than one.

TODAY'S SPECIALS!

Write the plural forms for these words.

bean _____   celery _____

squash _____   rice _____

beet_____   tea _____

WHOSE WHAT?

On the line under each picture, write a phrase that labels the picture. Make the first noun show possession.

(MOUSE, TAIL)

(BABY, CRY)

(SALLY, BLOOMERS)

(GOOSE, FEATHERS)

(WITCH, BREW)

(ESKIMOS, NOSES)

(FAIRY, WAND)

(JOGGER, NUMBER)

(THIEF, GLOVE)

Choose one phrase that is fun to think about. On the back of this page, write a short story about that idea. Use at least one possessive noun in each sentence of your story.

PRECISELY, MY DEAR

Look at each picture below. In the first space provided by each one, write a noun from your own vocabulary which you feel accurately describes the idea or feeling in the picture.

Now, look at the words written upside down at the bottom of this page. Assign each one to the picture which you feel it best labels or describes. (Use your dictionary to determine accurate word meanings.)

lunacy, paranoia, fantasy, security, sentimentality, clemency

COMIN' ON STRONG!

In the broadcasting world, information is sent by signal. The stronger the signal, the farther the message can be sent.

A writer's vocabulary is like a broadcast signal. The stronger it is, the farther the writer is likely to reach with a message.

Strengthen your signal by finding as many precise synonyms for these overworked words as possible.

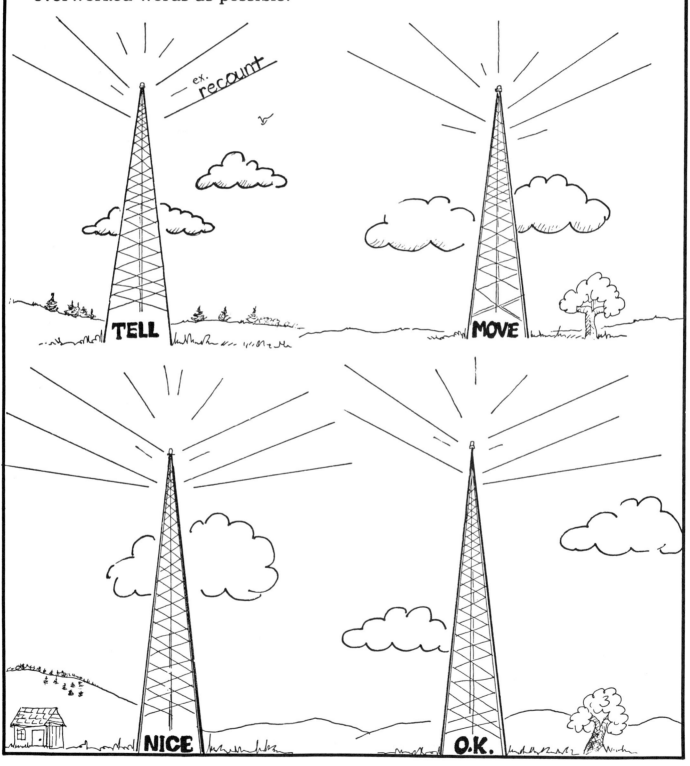

Choose 3 words from the list. Write each on a signal tower. Then, write words of your own on the remaining 2 towers. Strengthen your signals by "beaming" synonyms for all 5.

awful
good
thing
thought
dumb
tired
bad
super

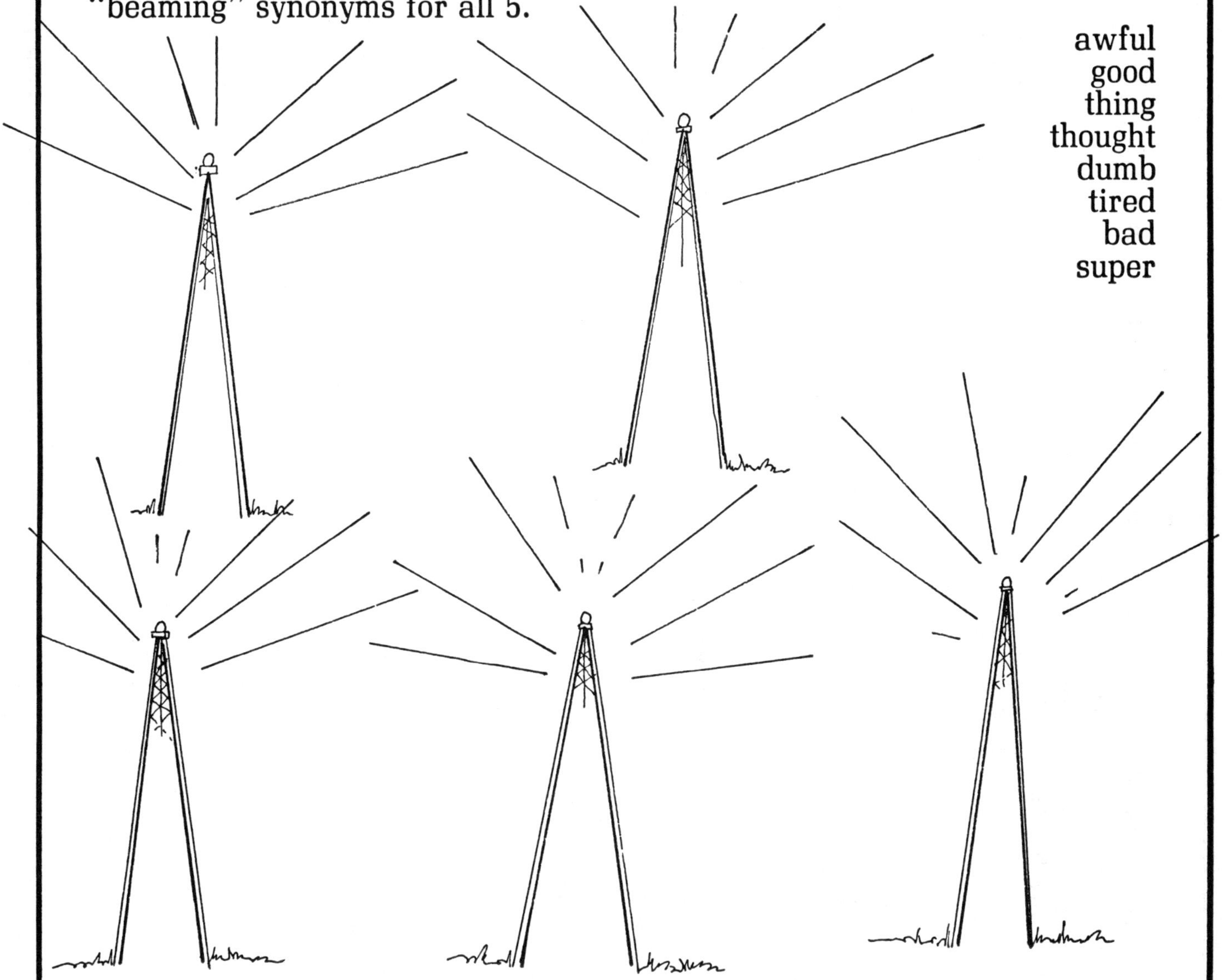

Use the spaces below to write 5 super sentences using one synonym from each tower. In each sentence, underline the synonym you have used.

1. _____

2. _____

3. _____

4. _____

5. _____

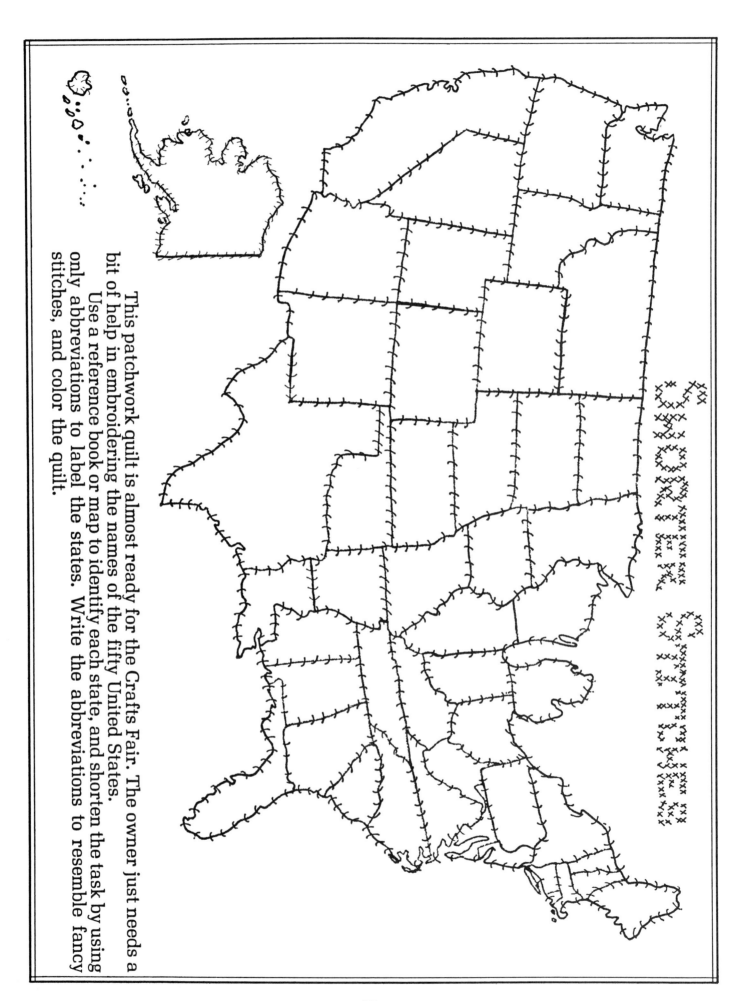

This patchwork quilt is almost ready for the Crafts Fair. The owner just needs a bit of help in embroidering the names of the fifty United States.

Use a reference book or map to identify each state, and shorten the task by using only abbreviations to label the states. Write the abbreviations to resemble fancy stitches, and color the quilt.

CONTRACTI' MAGIC!

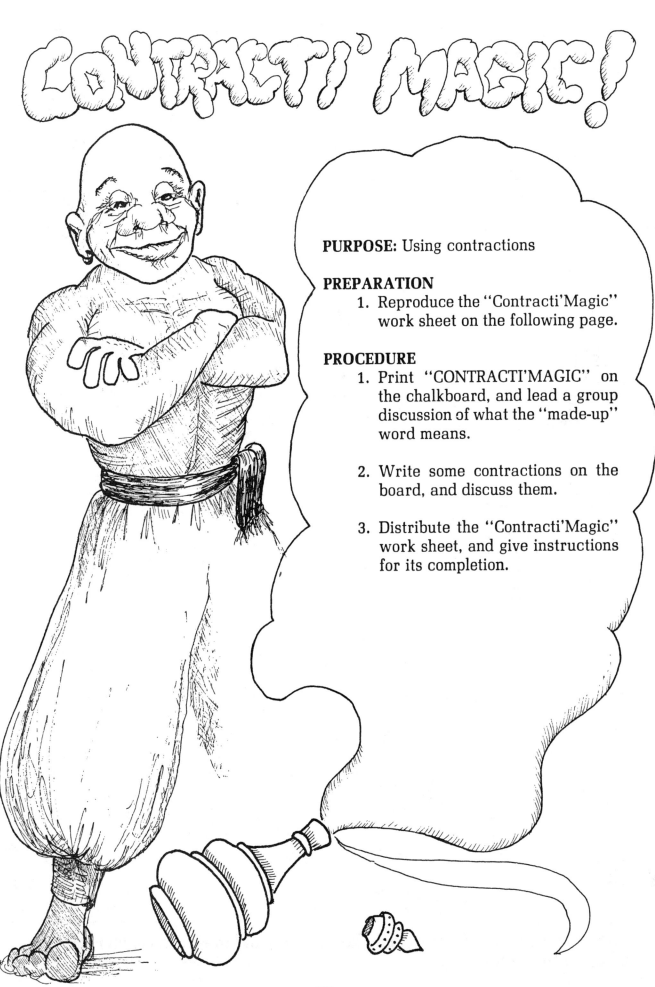

PURPOSE: Using contractions

PREPARATION
1. Reproduce the "Contracti'Magic" work sheet on the following page.

PROCEDURE
1. Print "CONTRACTI'MAGIC" on the chalkboard, and lead a group discussion of what the "made-up" word means.

2. Write some contractions on the board, and discuss them.

3. Distribute the "Contracti'Magic" work sheet, and give instructions for its completion.

List all contractions (there should be 16 in all) and the words each replaces on a separate sheet of paper.

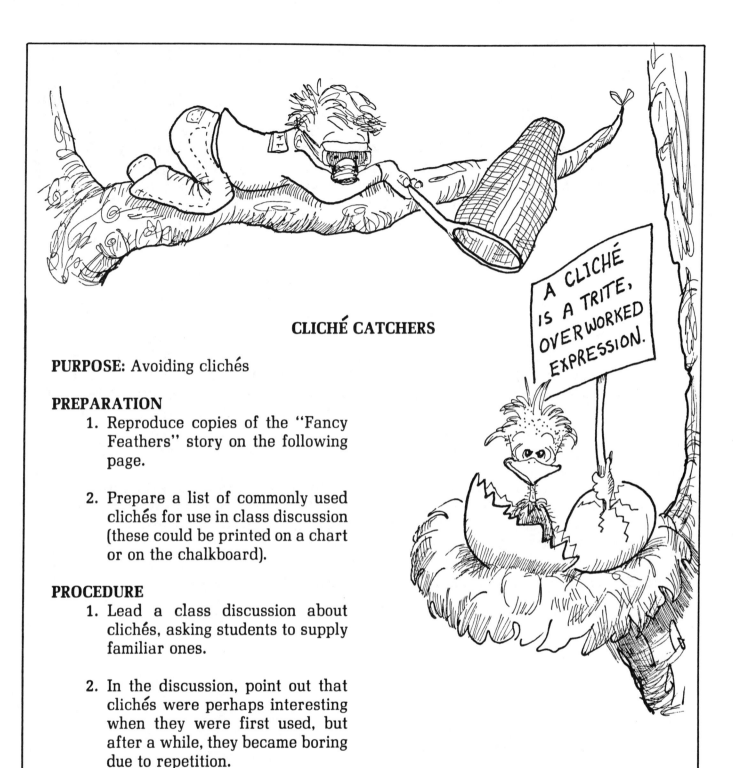

CLICHÉ CATCHERS

PURPOSE: Avoiding clichés

PREPARATION
1. Reproduce copies of the "Fancy Feathers" story on the following page.

2. Prepare a list of commonly used clichés for use in class discussion (these could be printed on a chart or on the chalkboard).

PROCEDURE
1. Lead a class discussion about clichés, asking students to supply familiar ones.

2. In the discussion, point out that clichés were perhaps interesting when they were first used, but after a while, they became boring due to repetition.

3. Distribute the "Fancy Feathers" story, and direct students to circle all the clichés in the story.

4. After the clichés have been circled, direct students to work in small groups (no more than 4 or 5 in a group) to rewrite the story, avoiding clichés by using more interesting figurative language. One student in each group should be appointed secretary to write the story as others discuss and dictate.

5. Display the completed stories on a bulletin board, or share them orally to demonstrate differences in language usage and writing styles.

FANCY FEATHERS

Betsy Bluebird was as snug as a bug in a rug living with her mother and three sisters. She preened and strutted as if her beautiful feathers had surely cost a pretty penny. In fact, old Mr. Owl said she behaved as if she had been born with a silver spoon in her mouth.

Early one morning, while flitting from bush to bush, she met Robin Red Breast, a dashing, fine feathered friend. He immediately invited her to tea by saying, "Come out, come out, little bird, as I feel that a bird in the hand is worth two in the bush."

Since they were able to see eye to eye, they immediately fell head over heels in love. They vowed to stick together through thick and thin, and to face the music of life together. Robin Red Breast said he would leave no stone unturned in his attempt to make Betsy Bluebird happy, and she promised to lend an ear always when he needed a friend.

Their first problem arose when he suggested that they kill two birds with one stone by building their nest in Robin Red Breast's territory while they were still young and smart as a whip. Betsy Bluebird began to cry crocodile tears and said her mother had always told her that birds of a feather flock together, and she really wanted to feather her nest near other bluebirds.

After much discussion, they finally came to a meeting of the minds, and decided to compromise by building their first nest in a halfway tree. They agreed to get started right away and let no grass grow under their feet since time flies, even for love birds!

You should have circled 19 clichés. How many did you miss? _____

A WRITING BEE

PURPOSE: Vocabulary development

PREPARATION

1. Gather the following materials.

    —scissors
    —construction paper
    —straws
    —masking tape
    —paper and pencils
    —dictionaries

2. Use the pattern to create a large number of "bees."

3. On each bee, write one descriptive word suitable to the level of the students.

4. Use masking tape to attach each bee to a drinking straw as shown.

PROCEDURE

1. Give each student a bee.

2. At a given signal, students send the bees into flight, tossing them into the air like paper airplanes.

3. When the bees land, each student picks up the nearest bee, reads the word on it, and writes a sentence using that word appropriately.

4. At the next signal, all bees are again sent into flight.

5. Repeat this procedure until the students have had opportunity to use at least 8-10 words.

NOTICING NOISEMAKERS

Circle at least ten noisemakers in this picture.

On the lines below, write one word for the sound each noisemaker might make. Be as imaginative as possible.

1._____   6. _____
2._____   7. _____
3._____   8. _____
4._____   9. _____
5._____   10. _____

On a separate sheet of paper, write a paragraph describing the street scene. Use each of the "noisemaker" words in the paragraph.

A MANY SPLENDORED THING

PURPOSE: Internalizing word meanings

PREPARATION

1. Tear sheets of multi-colored tissue paper into bits and pieces—the more shapes, sizes, and colors, the better. Maintain a free-form style with torn edges and no uniformity. Place the pieces in a basket or box.

2. Reproduce the "A Many Spendored Thing" work sheet, and distribute it to the students along with glue and the following directions.

PROCEDURE

1. Close your eyes, reach into the basket, and take a good handful of paper bits.

2. Using only the bordered space on the "A Many Splendored Thing" work sheet, arrange the paper bits to make a design. Let your imagination run free, and create the most original design possible before you glue it into place.

3. Look at you design. Give it a creative title, and list ten descriptive words and/or phrases that the design brings to mind.

4. Now, use some or all of your descriptive words and phrases to write a song, a poem, or a story to go with your design.

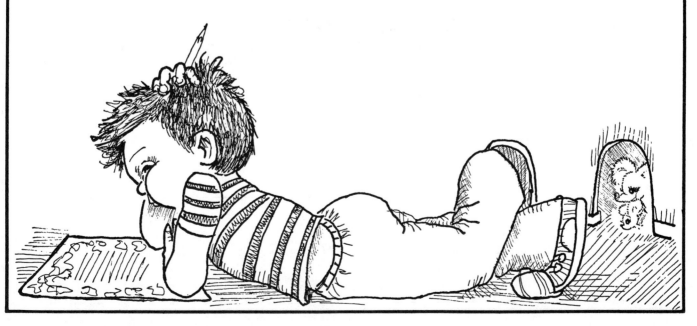

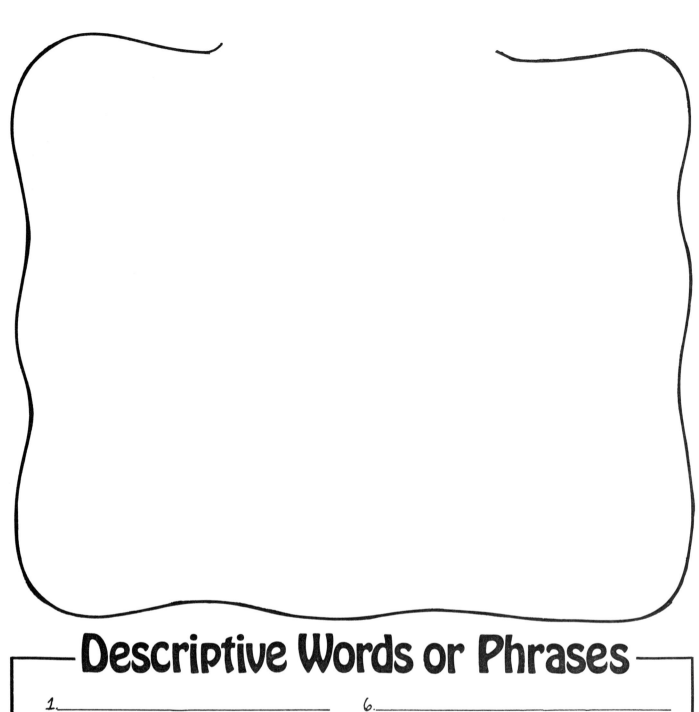

Descriptive Words or Phrases

1. _____
2. _____
3. _____
4. _____
5. _____
6. _____
7. _____
8. _____
9. _____
10. _____

What's in The Bag?

PURPOSE: Finding alternatives for overworked words

PREPARATION
1. At the beginning of the week, decide with the students on a day for this activity to be presented.

PROCEDURE
1. Each student brings one common household object of his/her choice to school in a small brown paper bag. The student's name should be written on the bottom of the bag so that it does not show.

2. Place all bags in a row.

3. Each person takes one bag, looks inside and makes a list of five words (single words only, no phrases) that can be used to describe the object in the bag and/or tell what it is used for.

4. One person then holds the bag closed before the group and gives the five words. Other group members try to guess what the item is. The person who guesses correctly gets the next turn. (It's fun when even the person who brought the item can't guess "What's in the Bag!")

S-T-R-E-T-C-H
a
Sentence!

PURPOSE: Finding alternatives for over-worked words

PREPARATION

1. Divide the class into two evenly-matched teams.

PROCEDURE

1. The first person on each team makes up a three-word sentence, and recites it loudly and clearly.

2. The second person on the team then repeats that three-word sentence. If he/she does so accurately, the student then adds a fourth word anywhere in the sentence, and recites that four-word sentence aloud.

3. The third person repeats the four-word sentence and then adds a fifth word. The activity continues in this manner until all team members have had a turn. (If a team member is unable to repeat a sentence, that turn is lost.) The team with the highest number of words in one sentence wins.

Here are 10 tired, worn-out adjectives that need to be replaced by fresh, alive, more exact ones. Select one or two substitute words from the middle column for each of the worn-out words in italics. Write the new adjectives you have selected for each word in the spaces provided.

1. *great* idea	splendid	1)_____idea
	helpful	
2. *nice* feeling	noble	2) _____feeling
	profitable	
3. *cute* girl	first-rate	3) _____girl
	dreadful	
4. *terrible* accident	disagreeable	4) _____accident
	peculiar	
5. *bad* storm	loyal	5)_____storm
	horrendous	
6. *fine* friend	delightful	6)_____friend
	frightening	
7. *funny* noise	strange	7) _____noise
	superb	
8. *big* house	terrific	8) _____house
	matchless	
9. *good* look	unpalatable	9) _____book
	expansive	
10. *awful* food	cherished	10)_____food
	satisfying	
	grand	
	superior	
	sensational	
	magnificent	
	colossal	
	attractive	

On the back of this paper, write a paragraph describing a person, a place, an object, or an experience. Do not use any of the ten adjectives in the first column.

Do You SPEAK SPORTS?

A NO-HITTER!

HE'S GROUNDED OUT!

He has 3 R.B.I's

He's EDGED HIM OUT!

It's a GRAND SLAM!

Many areas of interest have their own special jargon (or group of vocabulary words). In writing about these things, a writer must be able to use this jargon skillfully and accurately.

Each illustration below suggests an area of interest that has its own special jargon. Fill the spaces provided with as many of these related words as possible. (Encyclopedias, dictionaries, magazines, and books related to these topics will be of great help.)

1. Draw a line through the words that are not nouns.

girl	bet
grow	eat
house	crow

2. Draw a line under the word that is not a verb.

count	sense
crack	pet
under	mark

3. Circle each word that could be used both as a noun and a verb.

punch	nail
sneeze	pizza
speak	duck

4. Draw a line from each noun to the adjective that describes it.

tree	cloudy
bear	tall
day	furry

5. Circle all the adverbs that could modify the verb sniff.

carefully	often
short	tickly
quietly	suddenly

6. Each word in Column I can be at least 2 different parts of speech. Draw a line from each word to at least 2 appropriate words in Column II.

body	noun
clown	verb
name	adjective

7. Draw a line through each incorrect entry in the table below

Word	soar	none
Synonym	fly	all
Antonym	flew	nothing
Homonym	sore	nun

8. Cross out one word in each column that is not an acceptable meaning for the first word in that column.

back	take
behind	capture
move away	bother
hit	receive

9. Number the words in each column from 1 to 3 from the least to the most.

__ longer	__ peaceful
__ long	__ most peaceful
__ longest	__ more peaceful

10. Write the plural form of each of the following words.

    fox _____

    chief _____

    child _____

    man _____

11. Underline the group of words in each line that demonstrates the correct possessive form.

the mice's tails	the mouse's tails
Shirleys bag	Shirley's bag
babies rattle	baby's rattle
the men's room	the men's room

12. Circle the word in each group that most precisely describes the accompanying noun.

    tree—big, tall
    person—nice, generous
    food—good, spicy

13. Underline the abbreviations in this paragraph. Circle the contractions.

    Jeffrey awoke at 7 o'clock, MST. He checked the thermometer outside his window. It showed 20°F. "I won't be spending much time outside today!" he thought. Then he jumped out of bed to wash and dress. It wasn't 5 min. before he was ready, and he raced down the stairs. His family and Mr. Toby from next door were already at the table. "You're too quick for me," laughed Jeffrey. "I'm running a little late this morning." "I don't think so," said his mom. "We're just early because Dr. Thomas is picking up your dad. They're going to the U.S.A.F. meeting in Boulder, Colo., and they can't be late." Jeffrey didn't get a chance to ask if Gen. G. S. Gorham would be there, for just then a car pulled into the driveway, and his father ran out the door. "I'll be late, so don't wait up," called his father. "Goodbye!"

14. Circle the phrases you would not find in a precisely written news report.

    quick as a wink
    was criticized harshly
    received an unexpected visit
    killed two birds with one stone
    appeared to be under attack

15. Place the letter before each phrase in the blank beside its best match.

    A. hit a grand slam
    B. a fascinating thought
    C. superb, sensational
    D. a diabolic scheme
    E. went in for a lay up
    F. up a creek
    G. a personable old man
    H. dreadful, unpalatable
    I. a real scoop
    J. delightful, attractive.

    __ alternatives for "terrible"
    __ alternative for "interesting idea"
    __ basketball jargon
    __ alternatives for "great"
    __ jargon for news
    __ baseball jargon
    __ alternatives for "fine"
    __ alternative for "a nice elderly person"
    __ slang for "in trouble"
    __ alternative for "bad plan"

SKILLSTUFF

Using Technical Writing Skills

USING PUNCTUATION MARKS

_____ End Punctuation

_____ Commas

_____ Apostrophes

_____ Quotation Marks

_____ Colons and Semicolons

_____ Parentheses

USING CAPITAL LETTERS

SPELLING

WRITING SENTENCES

_____ Four Kinds of Sentences

_____ Writing a Good Sentence

_____ Fragments, Complete Sentences

_____ Run-On Sentences

_____ Subject-Verb Agreement

_____ Sentence Structure

_____ Parallel Construction

WRITING PARAGRAPHS

_____ Writing Topic Sentences

_____ Organizing a Paragraph

IMPLEMENTING MULTIPLE WRITING SKILLS

That's the Way the Cookie Crumbles!

PURPOSE: Using punctuation

PREPARATION

1. Use a cookie tin as the activity container.

2. Make 24 construction paper cookies; 12 whole, perfect cookies and 12 "crumbled" ones.

3. Number the cookies, and write one of the sentences from the following page on each. On the back of each cookie, write information to make the activity self-checking.

4. Place the cookies, pencils, and paper in the tin, along with the following student directions.

PROCEDURE

1. Number your paper from 1 to 24.

2. Look at each cookie. Decide if the correct punctuation has been used. If so, write "correct" beside the number. If not, copy the sentence beside the number, and punctuate it correctly.

3. When you have recorded all 24 cookies, turn them over and check your answers. For every "whole" cookie you answered correctly, give yourself 2 points. For every "crumbled" cookie, give yourself 1 point.

P.S. A real cookie to be enjoyed during the activity would add a nice touch.

1. Cookies cookies cookies everywhere and not a one to eat

2. Have you any cookies for sale?

3. We baked two dozen cookies yesterday.

4. My baby sister ate all, three cookies.

5. We ate every single one of Bruce's chocolate chip cookies.

6. Bobby likes sugar cookies better than anything,

7. My aunt Enid makes the best ginger cookies in the world.

8. Which box of cookies do you want.

9. I'm selling cookies for my Girl Scout Troup.

10. I didn't mean to but I ate all the cookies

11. Eating too many cookies will make you sick!

12. Have you ever eaten carrot cookies?

13. I need flour brown sugar and eggs to make these cookies?

14. Don't you dare drop that tray of cookies,

15. Yick! These cookies are stale.

16. Where did you get those, orange cookies:

17. Marlin called, "Please bring me some cookies."

18. My mother said, "That I couldn't have any more cookies."

19. I saw Jason hide two cookies inside his shirt.

20. Oh no? Someone sat on my last two cookies?

21. "Polly want a cookie!" screamed the parrot.

22. If you don't eat dinner you can't have any cookies for dessert;

23. Have you ever dunked cookies in hot chocolate?

24. We're having hamburgers, salad, and cookies for lunch.

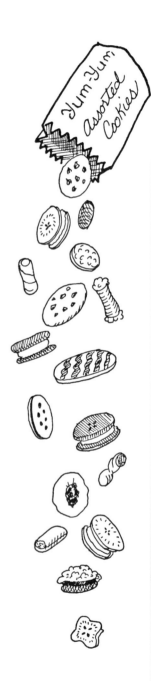

PUNCTUATION PIE

PURPOSE: Practice in using basic punctuation marks

PREPARATION
1. Use the illustration on this page as a model for creating several punctuation pies. (Pizza board or any similar heavy paper may be used.)

2. Cut each pie in pieces, and enter one punctuation mark on each piece. On the reverse side of each piece, write one or more sentences which require that punctuation mark. Then, add two long lines on which new sentences will be written.

PROCEDURE
1. "Serve" a piece of punctuation pie to each student.

2. Direct each student to use the mark on the top of that piece to punctuate the sentences on the back.

3. Then, direct students to add two original sentences that demonstrate the use of that punctuation mark.

SCRAMBLED PUNCTUATION

Unscramble the punctuation marks, and give a usage rule and an example for each one. Since the first one has been done for you, the same punctuation mark has been scrambled elsewhere on the page so that you can give another rule and example for its use.

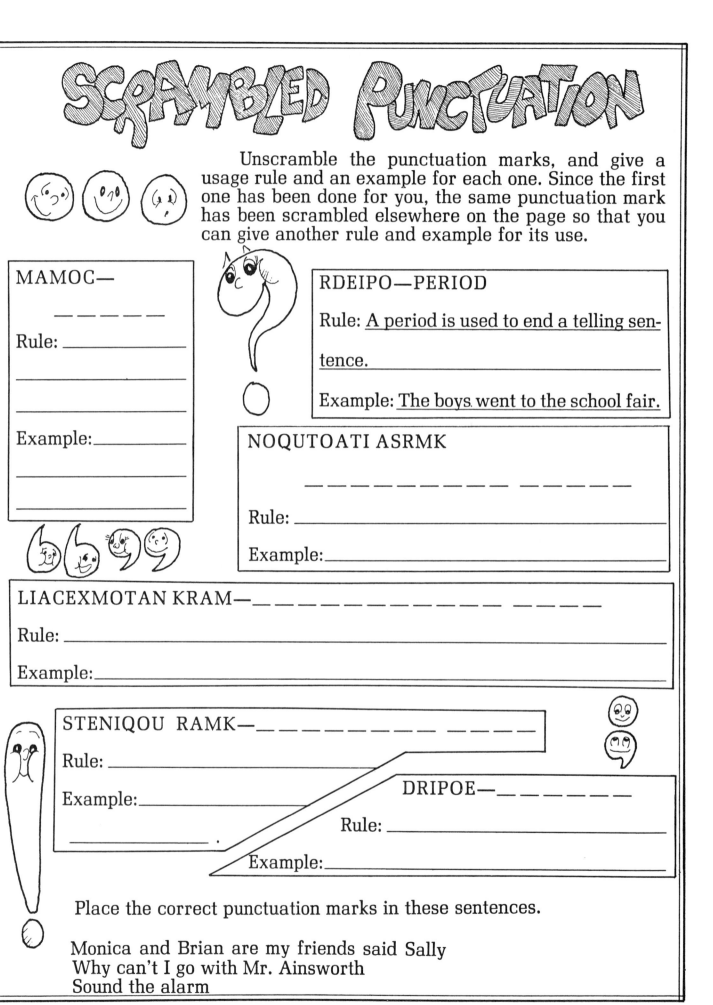

MAMOC—

_ _ _ _ _ _

Rule: _____

_____

_____

Example:_____

_____

_____

RDEIPO—PERIOD

Rule: <u>A period is used to end a telling sentence.</u>

_____

Example: <u>The boys went to the school fair.</u>

NOQUTOATI ASRMK

_ _ _ _ _ _ _ _ _ _ _ _ _ _ _ _

Rule: _____

Example: _____

LIACEXMOTAN KRAM—_ _ _ _ _ _ _ _ _ _ _ _ _ _ _

Rule: _____

Example:_____

STENIQOU RAMK—_ _ _ _ _ _ _ _ _ _ _ _ _

Rule: _____

Example:_____

_____ .

DRIPOE—_ _ _ _ _ _ _

Rule: _____

Example:_____

Place the correct punctuation marks in these sentences.

Monica and Brian are my friends said Sally
Why can't I go with Mr. Ainsworth
Sound the alarm

58

PURPOSE: Using capital letters

PREPARATION
1. Paste the following game board inside a manila folder.

2. Cut out the "Capital Bag" game cards. Paste the corresponding answer on the back of each card.

PROCEDURE
1. This game is for 2 to 4 players.

2. Place the game cards in the center of the board.

3. Each player selects a box car on the game board as "home base."

4. The first player takes the top game card from the stack, reads the sentence on it, and decides if proper use has been made of capital letters. (This includes both omitting capitals and/or using them in the wrong place.) If some capital letters are correctly used and others are not, the player must consider this an incorrect sentence.

5. The player then tells whether the sentence is correct or incorrect. If it is incorrect, the player must supply the correction.

6. The game card is then turned over for checking. If the player has given the correct information, the card is placed in his/her home base. If the player was incorrect, the card is placed at the bottom of the stack.

7. Players take turns continuing the game in this fashion until all cards have been used. The player with the box car holding the most "Capital Bag" game cards wins the game.

PURPOSE: Spelling practice

PREPARATION

    1. Gather the following materials.
          —Scrabble game
          —several sets of ABC building blocks

    Note: A large set of homemade letters (including apostrophes) on durable manipulative materials will add to or substitute for the above.

PROCEDURE

    1. When students have a group of spelling words which need to be reinforced, provide one or more of the above materials as the medium for practice in place of pencil and paper.

    (When using the Scrabble game or building blocks, designate a blank Scrabble chip or a picture block as an apostrophe.)

    2. Each student should be given opportunity to use each of the media at least once to spell the entire set of words. (For many students, this manual activity will reinforce the position of letters within words.)

    Note: If you have access to an outdoor signboard at a place of business, offer the proprietor the services of your class for changing the board regularly.

ADD A LITTLE COLOR

Lazy writers tend to use the same words over and over because it takes more effort to think of new or different ones. Have you ever found yourself using a word you knew how to spell rather than looking up another one in the dictionary?

Just to get started on an exciting approach to writing, use a dictionary or a thesaurus to find a more colorful word for each of the *italicized* words in the paragraph below. Recopy the paragraph with your replacement words in the space provided.

Thunder *roared* and lightning *flashed* in the *dark* sky. *Big* gusts of wind blew *large* tree branches and *loose* boards around the *old* house. *Dark* clouds gathered and began to *drop* rain on the *dry* ground, turning it into *brown* mud. An *old* man *ran up* *the wet* sidewalk to the *old* house. When he reached the *covered* porch, he turned around to *look* at the *big* storm. The rain was *coming* down in such *thick* sheets that he couldn't *see* the *curving* street in front of the house. He *looked* at the *heavy* rain and the *dark* clouds, and *wished* that the *big* storm would *go away*. Then he shook his head, opened the *heavy* door, and *went* quietly inside.

Compare the two paragraphs. List three additional words that could have been used somewhere in the paragraph to make it still more interesting.

THE WELL-SPELLED SCHOLAR

How are you as a speller? Really good, just o.k., a real loser, or absolutely fantastic? To find out, test yourself on the spelling list below. Read each word carefully to be sure you can pronounce it correctly and know its meaning. Look up any unfamiliar ones in the dictionary.

arctic	governor	library	picture	lightning
drowned	athlete	burglar	surprise	February
all right	biscuit	nickel	describe	history
every	attacked	popular	electric	extraordinary
separate	receive	expense	restaurant	generally
hoping	bargain	definitely	yesterday	colonel
shining	family	regular	usually	Wednesday
film	column	quiet	burst	chief

Now, record the spelling list on a tape recorder, dictating each word slowly and clearly. When the entire list has been recorded, play it back to yourself as a spelling test. Write the words on a piece of paper. Then, check your test paper by comparing it with this list. Place an X by each word that you missed, and study them carefully. Take the test again, and mark any missed words. Keep working until you are able to spell the entire word list. Use the study guide on the next page to help you.

When you have finished, look at the badges shown on the next page. Choose the one that best describes your progress, color it, cut it out, and pin it on yourself. Give yourself a pat on the back for your work!

HOW TO STUDY A SPELLING WORD

1. Look carefully at the whole word.
2. Be sure you understand its meaning.
3. Say it aloud, pronouncing each syllable distinctly.
4. Look at each syllable again to find expected trouble spots.
5. Shut your eyes and try to visualize the word.
6. Look at the word and write it, saying each letter as you write.
7. Write the word again without looking at your list.
8. Check to see that you've spelled it correctly.
9. Repeat all the steps until you've mastered each word.

WORD HIDE-OUT

PURPOSE: Reinforcing spelling

PREPARATION

1. Assign each student one spelling word from the week's list.

PROCEDURE

1. Ask each student to create a very short paragraph in which the assigned word is "hidden."

   Example: sense

   Captain Jensen sent an order to lessen secret activity in the enemy border. What he doesn't know is that Colonel Klink will erase 'n send it back.

2. Then, ask students to use at least 10 spelling words to create a word-find or crossword puzzle.

Example:

a	o	c	d	e	f	g
h	p	l	e	a	s	e
s	e	i	a	v	j	k
e	r	a	s	e	l	m
n	o	t	e	s	n	o
s	p	o	d	o	r	q
e	a	r	t	h	r	s

MEET THE FANTASTIC FOUR!

Permit me to introduce to you . . .

"DECLARATIVE CLEO"
The News Announcer

"INTERROGATIVE ROBERT"
The Computerized Robot

"IMPERATIVE PETE"
the Polite Policeman

"EXCLAMATORY CLARA"
the Chubby Cheerleader

Declarative Cleo speaks only in statements.
Her sentences end with a period.

Interrogative Robert speaks only in questions.
His sentences always end with a question mark.

Exclamatory Clara always shows surprise or strong feeling.
Her sentences end with an exclamation point.

Imperative Pete gives commands.
Usually, his sentences end with periods. However, if they show excitement, they might end with an exclamation point.

Cut out each sentence below. Read it carefully, and write in the correct punctuation at the end of the sentence.

Decide which one of the Fantastic Four would have spoken this sentence. Then, paste it on the appropriate space on the next page.

This is WGRP in Gallopogus, Georgia

That can't be true

Are you positive

Jumpin' jelly beans

What will happen next

Don't move

Do I have to

I certainly will not

Pick up your hat

I can't

Are you crazy

I'm falling

Only polar bears like cold water

It's freezing

Get out, right now

I think I'm asleep

What time is it

I have to go now

Look out

Where is my sweater

A SPORTING AFFAIR

PURPOSE: Writing a good sentence

PREPARATION
1. Provide paper and pencils for the participants.

PROCEDURE
1. Select a sport in which the students are interested. Lead a group discussion about the sport, and list ten descriptive words and ten action words from the discussion on the chalkboard.

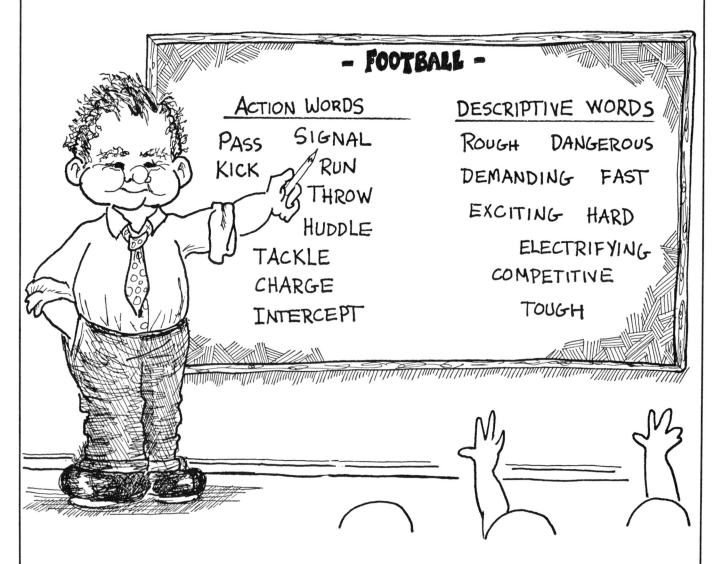

2. Direct students to write ten sentences about the sport. Each sentence must contain one action word and one descriptive word.

CUT AND CONCOCT

PURPOSE: Constructing sentences

PREPARATION

1. Make a copy of the following activity pages for each student or group of students.

2. Using a set of cards, show students how many combinations of the cards may be used to construct sentence stories.

3. Explain that the blank cards are to be filled in by the students with their original phrases.

PROCEDURE

1. Cut out the picture cards.

2. Choose a card that tells who or what the sentence will be about.

3. Then, choose one card (or more) that tells what this person or thing does.

4. Add another card (or cards) that tells what happens as a result.

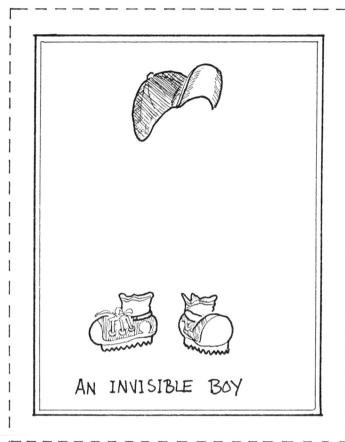

AN INVISIBLE BOY

ATE A JAR OF JAM

A BULBOUS LADY

WHILE TAKING A SHOWER

AND FLEW AWAY ON A GOOSE

A NERVOUS BURGLAR

A-A-A-A-CHOO!!

SNEEZED

CAUSING THE SKY
TO FALL

A PIGEON-TOED PENGUIN

AND EXPLODED

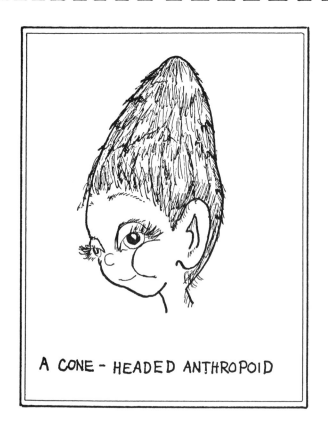

A CONE-HEADED ANTHROPOID

DRESSED UP LIKE A PEANUT

SENTENCED TO THINK

A sentence expresses a complete thought and should always make sense.

To solve the puzzle and find the hidden word, read the sentences and phrases below. If the words form a complete sentence, add the correct end punctuation, and color in the spaces in the puzzle that show that number. If the words do not form a complete sentence, move on to the next line.

1. And so we were

2. We were so tired

3. How are you

4. My mother and I

5. Turnips are good for you

6. Andrew was here

7. The big fat crocodile

8. Oh you frightened me

9. Please don't do that

10. Houses in the shade

11. The sun is setting

12. Moonlight and roses

13. Is the cook here

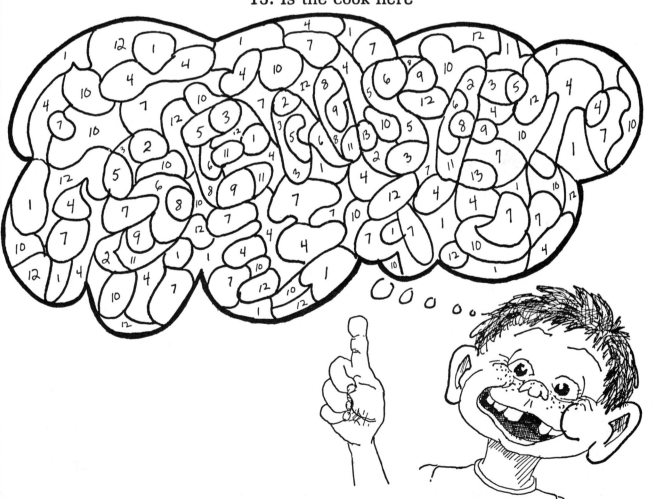

SOME GOOD NEWS, SOME BAD NEWS

Cut out the sentence strips from page 2 of this activity. Snip the run-on sentences apart to make two complete sentences, and add the correct punctuation to each. Decide whether each sentence is "Good News" or "Bad News," and paste it in the appropriate section of this page.

"Throw away" the incomplete sentences by pasting them on the trash can!

Today is my birthday I have the mumps

Once a huge monster

I caught a fish it was dead

A very important meeting with the committee

I'm invited to a swimming party there's a hole in my suit

If the biggest fish should get away

A roach as big as a bus

My best friend is having a pizza party I hate pizza

Mom gave me a big piece of cake my brother got a bigger one

I did three pages of math they were the wrong pages

I got to see a giant shark he was just three feet away

Any silly old scrap of paper

If I were going to run away

I can run a mile I can't jump far at all

When I was listening to the radio

RUN-ON TRACK

PURPOSE: Identifying and correcting run-on sentences

PREPARATION
1. Cut out the following game board. Paste the two pieces side by side on a large piece of cardboard.

2. Cut out the stop signs, the runners, and the stands. Glue stop signs to tops of bottle caps. Paste runners and stands on cardboard and cut out.

3. Copy the following Procedure directions on a small piece of cardboard. Place this, along with runners and stop signs, in a small zip-lock bag. Attach the bag to the game board.

PROCEDURE
1. This game is for 2 to 4 players.

2. Choose a runner and place it on the "Starting Line" of one running lane.

3. The first player throws the die and moves his/her runner the designated number of spaces. The player then reads the words in the spaces he/she has passed to determine if he has "run" a complete sentence. If he/she has passed a point at which a period should appear, the player must put a stop sign at that point.

4. If the player fails to identify that point, he/she must return to the position occupied before that turn. If the player does not complete a sentence, or if he/she has placed a stop sign appropriately, that player's turn is over and the next player takes a turn.

5. The first runner to reach the "Finish Line" wins the game.

Run-On Track Gameboard, p. 2

START

FINISH!

TICKETS

ATHLETES MUST BE STRONG THEY MUST KEEP THEIR BODIES IN GOOD

BEING A THREE-LEGGED RUNNER HAS ITS ADVANTAGES AND DISADVANTAGES OF

HOW WOULD YOU LIKE TO RACE BIG FOOT HOW GOOD ARE YOUR

HOW MUCH FUN IT WOULD BE TO BE BIONIC JUST THINK HOW FAST YOU

COULD LEAP TALL BUILDINGS

YOU BIONIC WERE IF YOU BURN OUT WHEN

BIONICS POWER TOO OF COURSE IF YOU

WERE REAL TWO-LEGGED ON ONLY LEFT GO TO ONE

SCARED OF HIM IT MIGHT HELP YOUR SPEED

IF WAIT TO BE A FINE ATHLETE YOU MUST

WERE A WINNING HARD WORK

RUNNER WHICH WOULD YOU PREFER TO BE?

IS NOT AS IMPORTANT AS FEELING GOOD

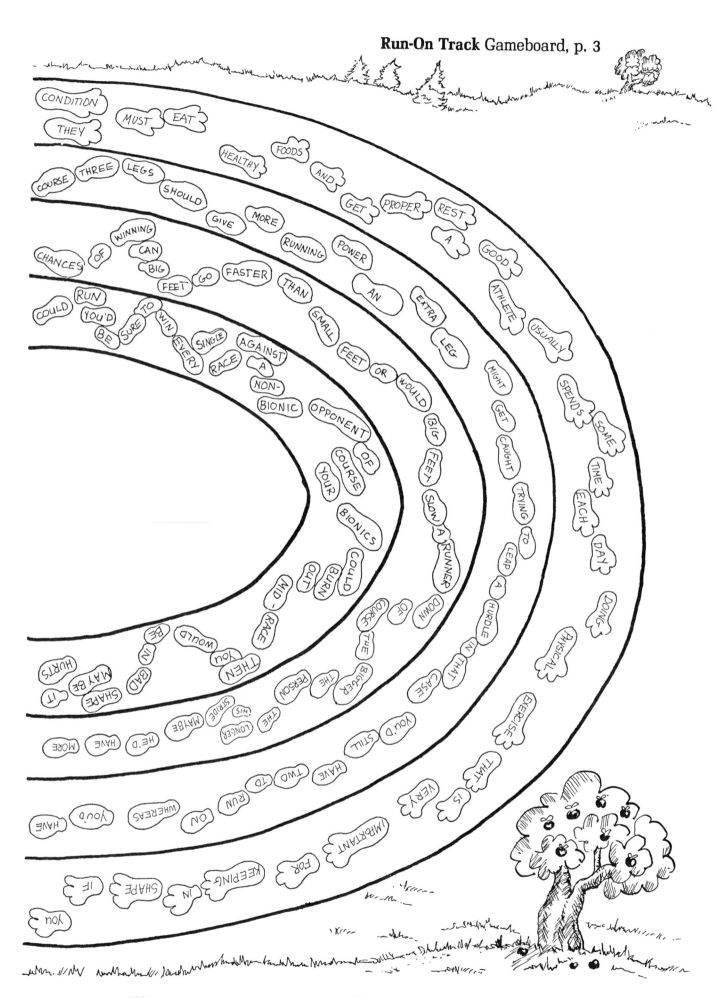

BREAKING THE CONJUNCTION CHAIN

Some people write sentences that just run on and on because they can't think how to divide the sentences to make shorter, more easily read sentences, and they tell too many things or convey too many thoughts. This style of writing becomes hard to read so the reader tends to just give up and refuses to try to get the message or even to read what has been written. Do you know anyone who writes run-on sentences and therefore confuses the issue and actually bores the reader, or worse still, do you write run-on sentences yourself?

Rewrite the paragraph above, dividing the sentences into shorter, more "readable" ones. Remember to present a complete thought in each sentence, and to use correct punctuation.

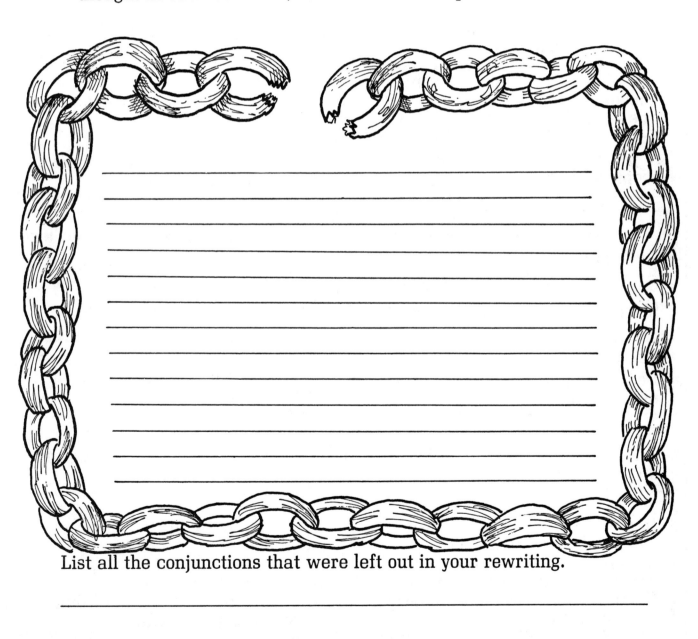

List all the conjunctions that were left out in your rewriting.

_____

_____

TO BUILD A FORT

Parallel construction means that the various parts of a sentence agree with each other.

This sentence is **not** parallel because the nouns which should agree in person do not:

A **person** should eat good food so **you** won't get sick.
3rd person   *2nd person*

However, both of the following sentences shown here are correct.

A **person** should eat good food so **he** won't get sick.
3rd person   *3rd person*

You should eat good food so **you** won't get sick.
2nd person   *2nd person*

Read the following sentence "logs." Decide which sentences are parallel in construction and which are not. Then follow the instructions on the second page of this activity.

A person should be polite so that people will like you.	Tom loves ham and eggs, and he eats them with catsup.
If you are sick, one should go to the hospital.	If you like apples, you would also like pears.
She is an actress, while he is a pilot.	She visited Grandma and then drove to see Aunt Maude.
Bears frighten me, but sharks scare me to death.	If you want to speak, you should raise your hand.
All kids eat ginger cookies because they like them.	Monsters come in several sizes and speak in several languages.
If anyone likes pie and cake, you should like ice cream, too.	Owls fly at night, but sleep in the daytime.
If a person eats a rotten hamburger, he will be sick.	No one should be afraid of thunder unless you are a baby.

Only sentences which are parallel in construction may be used to build this fort. Cut out those logs showing parallel construction, and paste each one of them on a part of the building. Load the faulty logs on the truck to return them to the lumber yard.

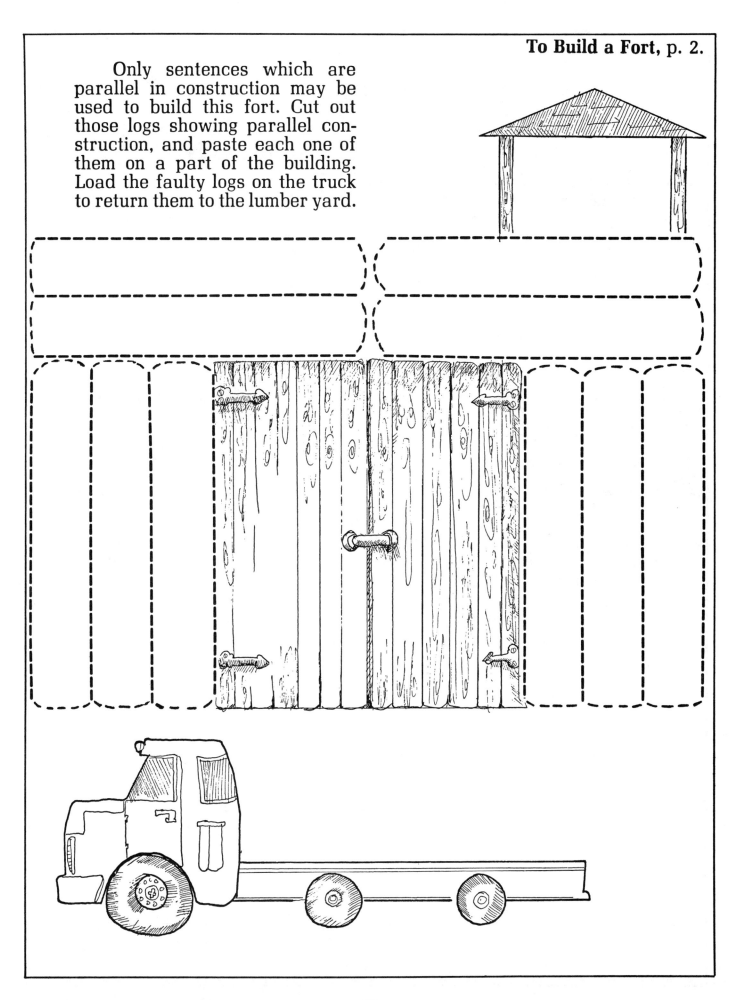

85

CHICKENS EVERYWHERE

VIC'S DELI

Write four different topic sentences that would make good beginnings for a paragraph that describes this funny picture. Then, choose the best one, and write a short paragraph about the event.

_____

_____

_____

_____

_____

_____

IDEAS IN ORDER

Number the sentences below to show the natural time order in which they occurred. Then, rewrite them in paragraph form in the space below. (Don't forget to indent the first line!)

___ Next, we tried to decide if we should go by air or by car.

___ Later, we agreed that all our time and effort had been well spent because this plan pleased both of us.

___ First, we spent hours making careful plans for our trip.

___ Then, we discovered this wonderful fly-and-drive package that allowed us to do both.

___ Meanwhile, we began collecting road maps and travel brochures.

___ Finally, the plans were complete, the bags were packed, and we were ready to go.

Write a paragraph telling about a trip you would like to take with your family.

SOME THINGS ARE HARD TO DESCRIBE

PURPOSE: Organizing a paragraph

PREPARATION
1. Provide paper and pencils for each participant.

PROCEDURE
1. Ask students to write a paragraph about something they "know" about but cannot see, smell, taste, touch, or feel. If necessary, lead a group discussion, and list some of these intangibles on the board.

   greed   tolerance
   youth   friendship
   peace   hate

2. Collect and save the completed paragraphs.

3. On the following day, ask students to write about something concrete. List some of the following on the board if examples are needed:

   coat   notebook
   tree   skyscraper
   chair   hamburger

4. Collect these paragraphs, and clip each student's papers together. Redistribute the paragraphs, and ask each student to make a line drawing at the bottom of each page.

5. Lead a class discussion on the difference in writing about tangible and intangible objects. Which is more difficult? Which makes one think more?

MASTERPIECE GALLERY

You are about to create an artistic masterpiece, using words and phrases as the images you will apply to your canvas.

You will need some old newspapers or magazines, scissors, paste, and a piece of heavy construction paper. Add a frame from another color of paper, if you like.

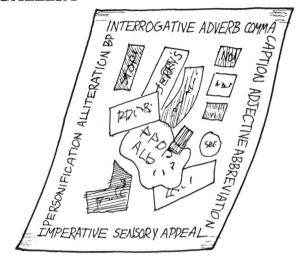

Find at least one example of each item listed below. Then, on your heavy paper, create a collage using the pieces you have collected.

When you have finished your collage, hang it where your classmates can see and enjoy your work.

a caption   a title showing alliteration   an adverb

an expletive   a phrase with a comma   a proper noun

a metaphor   an interrogative sentence   an abbreviation

a possessive noun   a cliché

a word unfamiliar to you (until now, of course)

an imperative phrase or sentence

a picture demonstrating personification

HIKE AND HUNT

PURPOSE: Using technical and creative writing skills

PREPARATION
1. Prepare students for a hike in the area immediately surrounding the school building (this may include getting written parental permission, review of safety rules, etc.).

2. Reproduce copies of the following pages. Be sure that each student brings these pages and a pencil on the hike.

PROCEDURE
1. Students follow the instructions given on the "Hike Log" pages to find or create words and phrases that fulfill each requirement.

2. At the end of the hike (or after additional class working time), collect the logs for evaluation by a committee, a classroom partner, or the teacher.

3. If all requirements have been fully and satisfactorily completed, a student may receive one day free of homework assignments, a free reading period or some other privilege designated by the teacher.

HIKE LOG

Each item below represents one or more requirements you must fulfill to be an expert "Language Hiker." Along the route of your hike, you will be expected to find many things. Enter your findings in the spaces provided.

If you complete each item successfully, you will be awarded a special privilege at the end of the trip.

Good luck!!

Hike and Hunt
for these things:

An exclamatory sentence about your hike.

A couplet expressing some feeling about your hiking adventure.

Headline or caption from some outdoor advertising using sensory appeal.

A sentence telling 4 things you saw (to demonstrate correct use of commas).

A map showing the route of your hike:

Four things or places whose names begin with capital letters: _____ _____ _____ _____

An interrogative sentence about something you saw: _____

A sentence or phrase demonstrating personification, using the season of the year as the personified object: _____

A limerick about your hike:

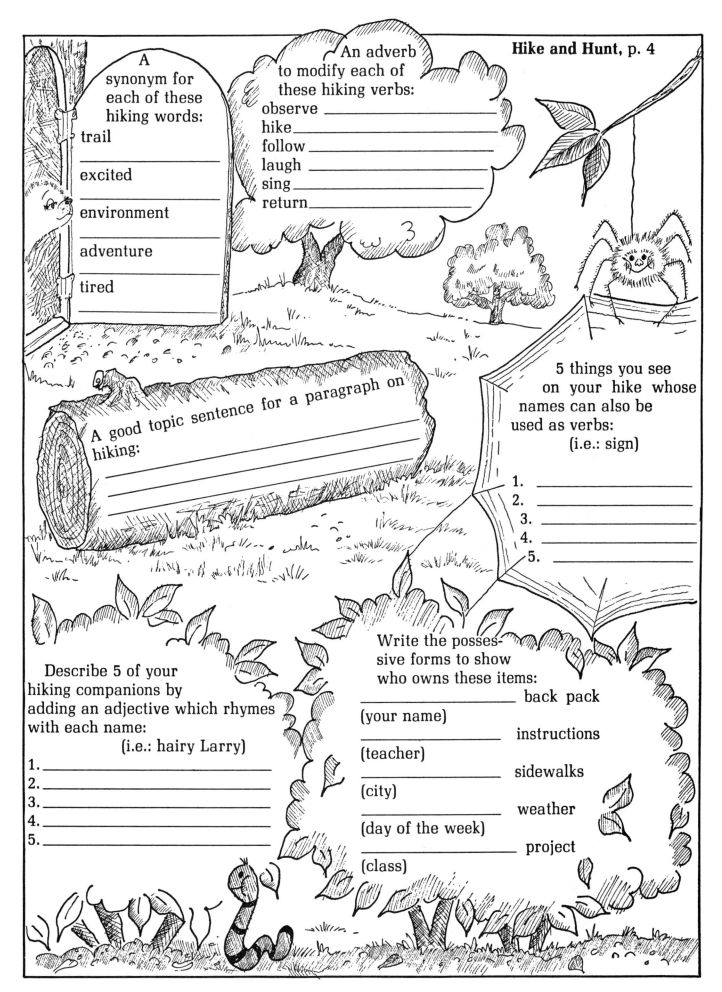

A synonym for each of these hiking words:

trail

_____

excited

_____

environment

_____

adventure

_____

tired

_____

An adverb to modify each of these hiking verbs:

observe _____

hike _____

follow _____

laugh _____

sing _____

return _____

A good topic sentence for a paragraph on hiking:

_____
_____
_____

5 things you see on your hike whose names can also be used as verbs:
(i.e.: sign)

1. _____
2. _____
3. _____
4. _____
5. _____

Describe 5 of your hiking companions by adding an adjective which rhymes with each name:
(i.e.: hairy Larry)

1. _____
2. _____
3. _____
4. _____
5. _____

Write the possessive forms to show who owns these items:

_____ back pack
(your name)

_____ instructions
(teacher)

_____ sidewalks
(city)

_____ weather
(day of the week)

_____ project
(class)

93

OH YES, I CAN!

PURPOSE: Writing sentences; using multiple meanings; using parts of speech

PREPARATION

1. Cover a coffee can or a potato chip can with white paper on which words familiar to the students have been printed.

2. Make 15 sets of cards with three words beginning with the same letter (45 cards in all). These and/or others may be used.

crayon	stop	dark	party	rate
cap	soup	draw	pink	roar
coop	spy	dent	plant	ripe
link	ask	bear	though	group
loop	always	blunt	thought	gate
letter	arrow	bank	through	gone
mother	old	in	zebra	jump
may	other	icicle	zoo	just
met	off	it	zinc	jet

Put the cards in the can.

3. Reproduce the study guides and work sheets, and place materials in a center.

PROCEDURE

1. Introduce the center to enable the students to complete the activities independently.

2. Arrange time for evaluation of each activity, and record individual student progress.

94

I CAN MAKE SENTENCES

1. DRAW CARDS FROM THE "WORD CAN" UNTIL YOU HAVE FIVE SETS OF THREE CARDS, EACH BEGINNING WITH THE SAME LETTER.

2. PLACE THE 5 SETS IN STACKS BEFORE YOU. MAKE A SEPARATE STACK OF ALL THE OTHER CARDS DRAWN.

3. ARRANGE THE THREE WORDS IN EACH OF THE FIVE SETS IN ALPHABETICAL ORDER.

4. ON THE "I CAN MAKE SENTENCES" WORKSHEET, MAKE ONE SENTENCE USING ALL THREE OF THE WORDS IN EACH STACK. TRY TO MAKE FUNNY OR INTERESTING SENTENCES. (USE YOUR DICTIONARY FOR HELP IN SPELLING WORDS).

5. PUT YOUR COMPLETED "I CAN MAKE SENTENCES" SHEET ON THE BULLETIN BOARD.

WORDS

SENTENCES

1. 1. _____
   2. _____
   3. _____

2. 1. _____
   2. _____
   3. _____

3. 1. _____
   2. _____
   3. _____

4. 1. _____
   2. _____
   3. _____

5. 1. _____
   2. _____
   3. _____

I CAN USE WORD MEANINGS

1. From the stack of cards you had left over, select all the words that you think have more than one meaning.

2. Make a new stack of the other cards. If you did not have at least three words with more than one meaning, draw from the word can until you have this many.

3. Look up each word in your dictionary. Write the word on the "I CAN USE WORD MEANINGS" worksheet, and draw pictures beside it to show two different meanings.

I CAN USE WORD MEANINGS

WORD

WORD

WORD

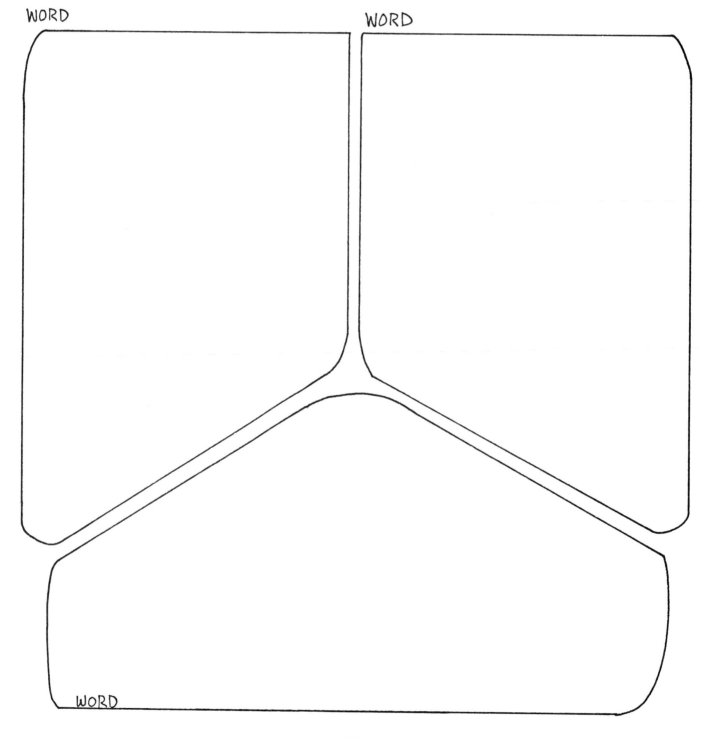

I CAN FIND PARTS OF SPEECH

1. ARRANGE THE CARDS IN THE LAST STACK IN ALPHABETICAL ORDER. IF YOU HAVE FEWER THAN TEN, DRAW ENOUGH FROM THE CAN TO MAKE TEN.

2. LIST THE WORDS ON THE "I CAN FIND PARTS OF SPEECH" WORKSHEET.

3. FIND EACH WORD IN YOUR DICTIONARY. BESIDE THAT WORD ON YOUR PAPER, CIRCLE EACH PART OF SPEECH IT CAN BE. THEN, WRITE A SENTENCE SHOWING EACH USE OF THE WORD.

I CAN FIND PARTS OF SPEECH

Word	Parts of Speech	Sentences
1) _____	noun adjective verb adverb other_____	_____ _____ _____
2) _____	noun adjective verb adverb other_____	_____ _____ _____
3) _____	noun adjective verb adverb other_____	_____ _____ _____
4) _____	noun adjective verb adverb other_____	_____ _____ _____
5) _____	noun adjective verb adverb other_____	_____ _____ _____
6) _____	noun adjective verb adverb other_____	_____ _____ _____
7) _____	noun adjective verb adverb other_____	_____ _____ _____
8) _____	noun adjective verb adverb other_____	_____ _____ _____
9) _____	noun adjective verb adverb other_____	_____ _____ _____
10) _____	noun adjective verb adverb other_____	_____ _____ _____

1. Place the proper punctuation marks in the blanks.

    ____ Horrors ____ Someone has stolen my hat ____ my gloves ____ and my wig __ __ said Horace LeBlanc. ____ Hasn__t anyone seen the thief ____ ____

2. In the paragraph below, draw a line through all the letters that are capitalized but should not be. Circle all letters that are not capitalized but should be.

    David's Birthday is in january. he will be Nine. His Mother is baking him a sesame street cake, and He will receive a monopoly game. His special guests will be grandfather and his friend joey.

3. Cross out the misspelled word in each pair.

    usualy, usually
    nickel, nickle
    populer, popular
    seperate, separate

4. Draw a line through the sentence that is not declarative.

    A bear ate my mittens.
    Do you know my uncle?
    I like you.

5. Circle the sentence that is imperative.

    Do you hear me?
    I'm being robbed!
    Stop that nonsense now!

6. Place the proper punctuation at the end of the interrogative sentence. Make no marks by the other sentences.

    I am a monster
    Are you a robot
    I can't believe it

7. Identify the problems below by placing the proper letter in the blank next to each.

    A—sentence fragment
    B—run-on sentence
    C—subject/verb disagreement
    D—unparallel construction

    ____ A penguin sneezed he died.
    ____ Had an unfortunate experience.
    ____ Ian and Ann has thirty cents.
    ____ All the cake in the world.
    ____ One should go to the doctor if you are sick.
    ____ The birds likes their house.
    ____ I'm going to town you can come, too.

8. Cross out the sentence that would not be a good topic sentence for the paragraph below.

    A kid should really have a pocket.
    A toad needs a pocket to be put into.
    Whoever heard of a kid without a pocket?

    Suppose a child is walking along a dirt road, kicking stones, and he finds a perfect one. What would he do with it, if he didn't have a pocket? A kid needs at least 7 pockets— one for stones, one for pennies, two for food, one for bugs, and two for hands.

9. Number the following entries in the order that you would place them in a well-organized paragraph.

   ___ The hump is convenient to sit upon.
   ___ I wonder if the camel minds very much being used by people in such a way.
   ___ He has a hump.
   ___ The camel is traditionally a beast of burden for man.
   ___ And incidentally, the camel is good for shading a person who stands next to it in the hot sun.
   ___ It is good for storing water for the camel's use.

10. Match each item in Column I with its best match in Column II.

Column I

   A. interrogative sentence
   B. use of commas in a series
   C. capitalization needed
   D. topic sentence
   E. imperative
   F. fragment
   G. misspelling
   H. apostrophe missing

Column II

   ___ Winters icy breath knocks me cold.
   ___ Unbeleivable!
   ___ spring paints green on everything.
   ___ Let's talk about toes.
   ___ Where are you?
   ___ toes with bells on them
   ___ There were sticks, stones, bottles, and boxes.
   ___ Shake yourself!

SKILLSTUFF

Composition & Original Writing

COLLECTING AND ORGANIZING IDEAS

____ Using a Variety of Resources
____ Sequencing Thoughts
____ Note Taking, Summarizing
____ Paraphrasing
____ Précis Writing

USING FIGURATIVE LANGUAGE

____ Metaphors and Similes
____ Personification, Alliteration, Onomatopoeia

USING SPECIAL LITERARY DEVICES

____ Sensory Appeal
____ Point of View
____ Puns
____ Emotional Appeal
____ Unusual Perspective
____ Imagery, Mood, Parody, Irony, Hyperbole

USING PROSE FORMS

____ Characterization
____ Description
____ Dialogue
____ Narrative
____ News Reporting, Editorials

USING POETIC FORMS

____ Rhymed (couplets, rhyme schemes, etc.)
____ Unrhymed (haiku, cinquain, quatrain, free
       verse, etc.)

WRITING TITLES, CAPTIONS, AND LABELS

EDITING AND PROOFREADING

PUTTING IT ALL TOGETHER

The following pages contain sample documents and personal references from the file of a person unknown to you, but one of whom you, as a police reporter, must write a description.

Look at the material carefully. Learn all you can from it, and then complete the two lists below.

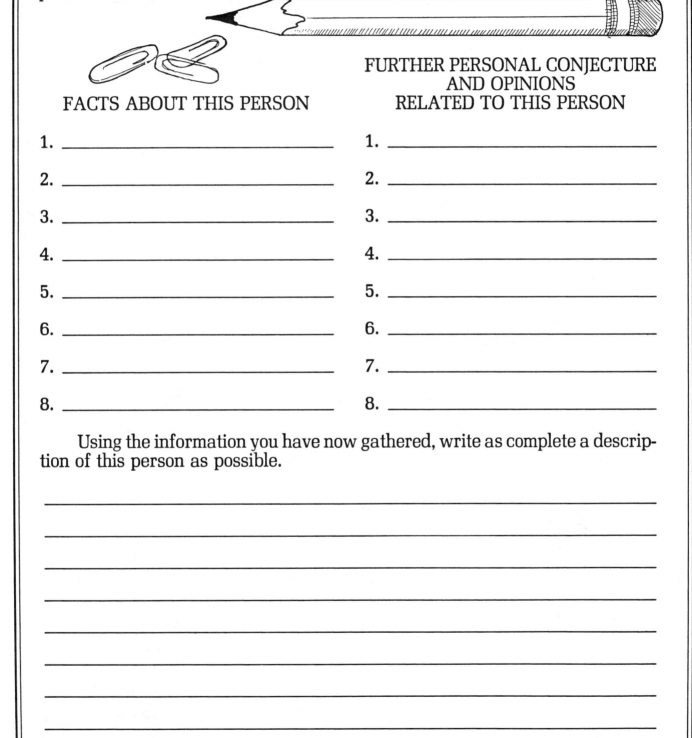

FACTS ABOUT THIS PERSON

1. _____
2. _____
3. _____
4. _____
5. _____
6. _____
7. _____
8. _____

FURTHER PERSONAL CONJECTURE
AND OPINIONS
RELATED TO THIS PERSON

1. _____
2. _____
3. _____
4. _____
5. _____
6. _____
7. _____
8. _____

Using the information you have now gathered, write as complete a description of this person as possible.

_____

_____

_____

_____

_____

_____

_____

_____

_____

MRS. ADELLE ASHCROFT
8 ASHBURY ALLEY
ADELAIDE, AUSTRALIA

Dear Abe,

I have tried for several years to locate you. Your brother Alex gave us your address in Africa, but our letter to you there was returned marked "unknown". We then traced you to Athens and Arabia and were told you had been in each place only briefly. It is good finally to have located your friend Asa in Atlanta and learnt that you were well.

We shall look forward to meeting you upon your return from Aruba.

Sincerely,
Adelle

APPLICATION FOR EMPLOYMENT

NAME _Adams_____ _Abe_____ _A.___   Soc. Security No. _888-000-888_
     Last   First   Middle Int.

Present Address _80 Allen Ave._____ _Anchorage_ _Alaska____ _99801_
               No.   Street   City   State   Zip

How long have you lived at present address? _6 mos.____ Phone _888-4838_

Previous Address _800 Ambrose Ave._ _Anderson_ _AZ___ _85079_
                 No.   Street   City   State   Zip

How long did you live there? _3 mos_

Date of Birth _8/8/38____   Place of Birth _Andalucia, Ala._

EDUCATION:

Elementary: Last grade completed _6_

High School: Last grade completed _12_

College: How many years completed? _6_ Date of completion _1962_

         Degree earned _M.A._____ Date of completion _____

         Degree earned _____ Date of completion _____

         College Major _For. Languages_ College Minors _English_
                                                         History
                                                         Psychology

Interests, hobbies or honors: _honors: Foreign language Award; Lang. Society_
President.   reading, traveling, backpacking, carpentry

106

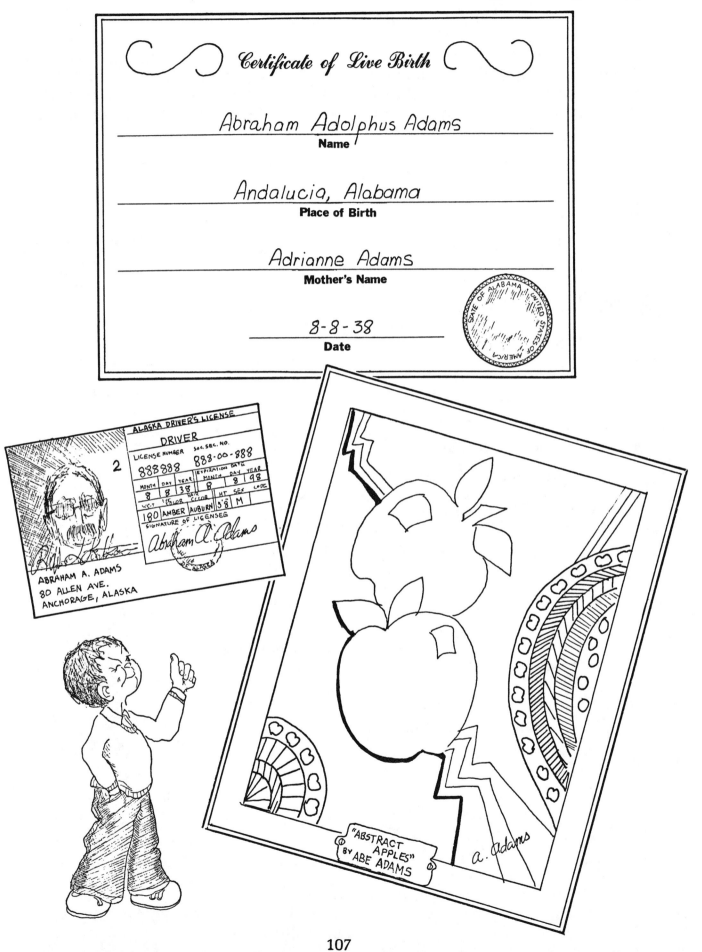

PART TO PART, FROM THE START

This is a story, but its parts are not in order. Read each part carefully. Then, beginning with the part that starts the story, draw a squiggle line to connect each part to the part that follows it until the whole story is connected.

BEWARE!! One part does not belong. Cross it out, and do not connect it at all!

_____
(Write your title here.)

This story is for you to write. Look at the pictures in all the parts. Decide which part should begin the story. Write the words for that part. Then, find the second part, and write the words for that part.

Keep going until you have finished the story. Then, connect the parts in order with a squiggle line so that your friends can read your story.

(Write your title here.)

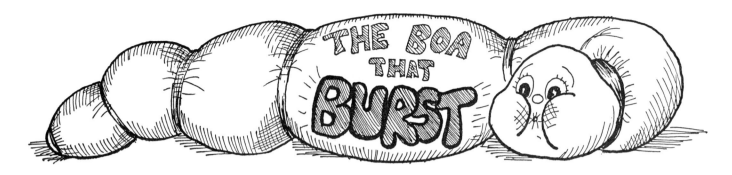

PURPOSE: Sequencing thoughts

PREPARATION

1. Write the following words (or choose 5 nouns and 5 verbs of your own) on the chalkboard in this order.

1. bus	6. burst
2. turtle	7. cried
3. coffeepot	8. danced
4. dictionary	9. flew
5. boa	10. crowed

2. Beneath these words, write:

    The _____ That _____

3. Cover this section of the board from the students' view.

4. Supply each student with paper and pencils.

PROCEDURE

1. Divide students into four or five groups.

2. Ask each student to choose a number between 1 and 5, and write it at the top of the paper. Then, ask each student to choose a second number between 6 and 10, and write that number beside the first number chosen.

3. Uncover the words on the board. Direct students to copy the title you placed on the board at the top of their papers, filling in the blanks with the words from the board that correspond to the numbers chosen.

    Example: If a student chooses numbers 5 and 6, the title will be "The Boa That Burst."

4. Each student then begins to write about his/her title. After a few minutes, a signal is given, and papers are passed to the right. Each story is then continued by the next student. This process is repeated until everyone in each group has contributed to each story. On the final pass, students must bring the stories to a conclusion.

5. Taking turns, each student reads aloud the story for which he has written the conclusion.

PRIVATE EYE

PURPOSE: Note-taking/summarizing

PREPARATION
1. See that each student has a small notebook and a pencil to be used only for recording observations.

PROCEDURE
1. Direct students to secretly and individually choose one classmate as a "suspect" to "tail" or keep track of—"on the sly," of course.

2. Explain to the students that they should carefully observe as many of the daily activities of this person as possible. Major movements, activities, and any information that he/she finds particularly interesting about the "suspect" should be recorded in the "Private Eye" notebooks.

3. After a specified amount of time, each "Private Eye" prepares a summary report on his/her "suspect" and reads it to the class. If the "suspect" recognizes himself or herself from the description, he/she may reveal his/her identity. If not, the class may guess the "suspect's" identity.

THE PARAPHRASE CRAZE

HASTE MAKES WASTE!!

Can you rephrase that (say it in different words without changing the meaning)?

Like this; Hurrying causes error.
Or, like this: If you hurry, you may make a mistake and have to start over, thus wasting time, energy, and materials.

Saying the same thing in different words is called paraphrasing. Usually, paraphrasing is done to make something more clearly understood.

Trade these "antique" phrases for some written in your own modern language. Read each of the sentences below, and paraphrase it. Then, write your parphrase on the matching, newer item.

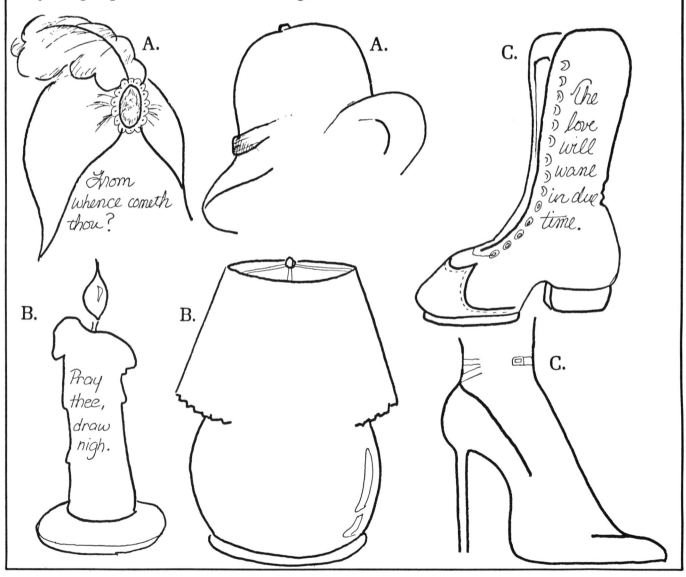

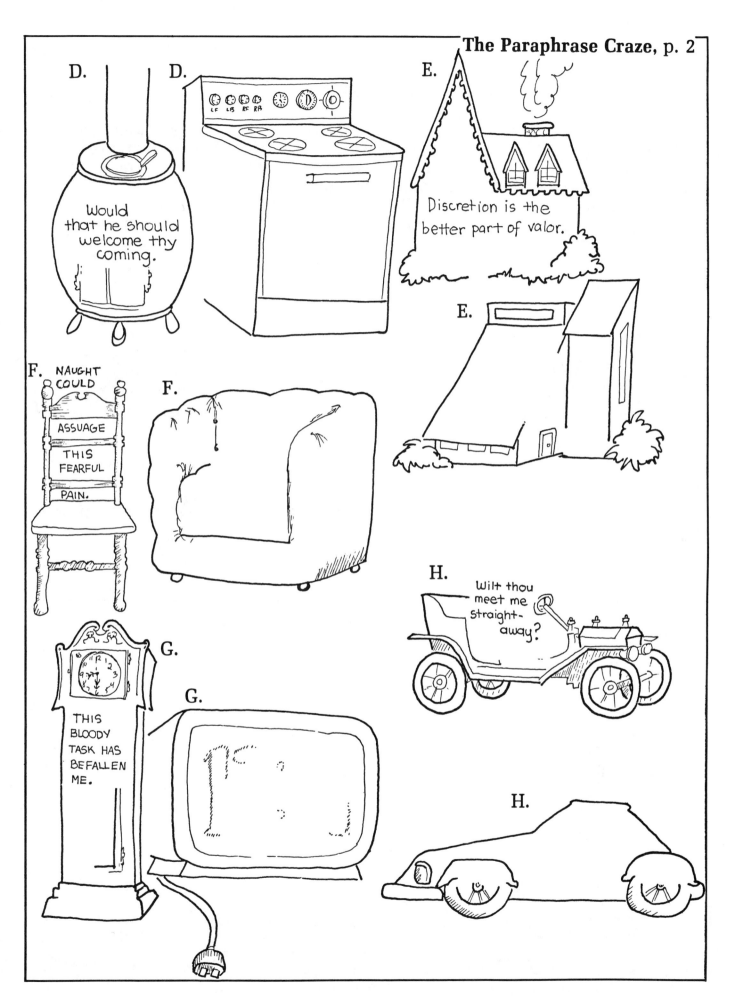

NEWSBEAT

Building the ability to "zero in" on just the most important facts of a story or news item is essential to good writing. The classified ad section of a newspaper is an excellent example of well-pared or "précis" writing style, because people pay for these ads by the line.

Read some newspaper ads. Then try to copy that style by writing a classified ad that you think would sell each of the items shown below. Pretend that it costs you $10.00 a line! See how few lines you can use and still describe each item fully, mentioning all the important details and pointing out the special features that will make people want to buy it.

your choice

As Smart As A Whip!

Are you? Prove it. See if your can complete these similes.

As fresh as a _____

As meek as a _____

As good as _____

As sly as a _____

As sweet as a _____

As clear as_____

As quick as a_____

As clean as a_____

As neat as a _____

As blind as a _____

As cool as a _____

As dead as a _____

As stubborn as a_____

As pale as a _____

As funny as a _____

As pretty as a _____

How did a whip get to be smart? In these spaces, copy four of your favorite similes from the list above. Beside each, write your guess as to how this simile came to be a common figure of speech.

_____ - _____

_____

_____ - _____

_____

_____ - _____

_____

_____ - _____

_____

In the two spaces below, make up some similes of your own.

CRACK!

_____

_____

115

JUKE BOX JARGON

Did you ever hear of the song, *Love Your Lazy Liver*, sung by Limp Lung and the Laplanders? No? Well, neither did anyone else. All that song has going for it is **a lot of alliteration.** (How about that?)

This juke box plays only hit songs with alliterative titles, sung by alliterative artists. The key buttons give you the initial sound for each record. You get to name the tunes and the artists. (Do the flip side of each record, too!)

UFO'S (UNIDENTIFIED FIGURES OF SPEECH!)

Concentrate your lazer-powered focus beam on these UFO'S to see if you can identify them with one of these friendly alien groups:

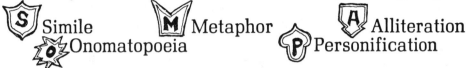 Simile Metaphor Alliteration
Onomatopoeia Personification

Mark each UFO with its identifying initial shield. (A few UFO'S may be members of more than one group!)

Using what you have learned on the first page of this activity, create additional FO'S to match each identifying shield shown here.

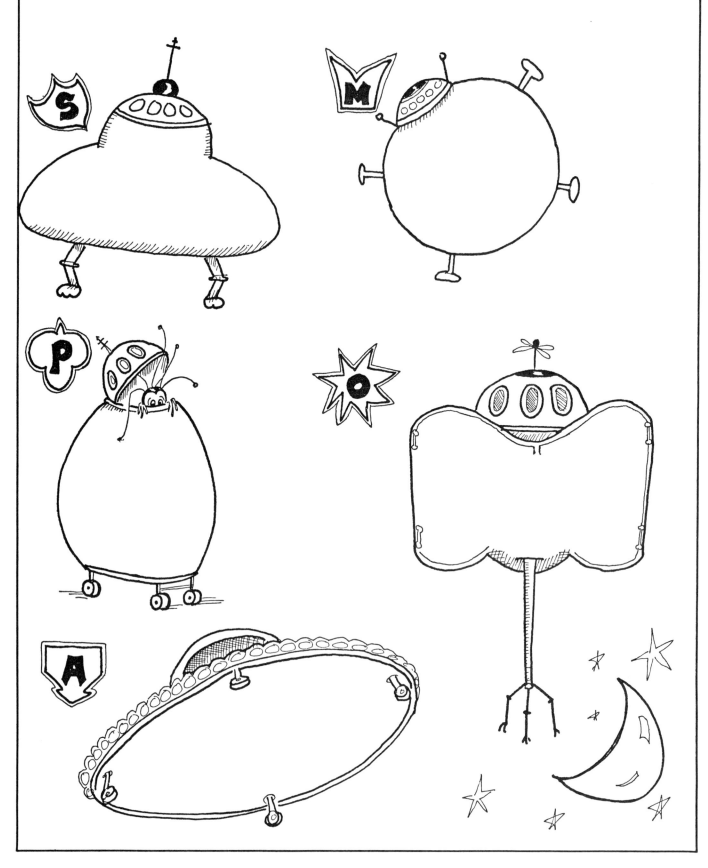

PURPOSE: Identifying figures of speech and literary terms

PREPARATION
1. Prepare 8 posters with one of the following titles on each:

Metaphor	Simile	Alliteration	Personification
Idioms	Puns	Hyperbole	Onomatopoeia

    Add at least one example to each poster as a "starter," and display the posters together on a large bulletin board.

2. Provide a stack of old newspapers and magazines. (*Sports Illustrated, McCall's, Ladies Home Journal, Seventeen,* and daily papers are especially good for this activity.)

3. Reproduce a copy of the "Literary Lingo" work sheet for each student.

PROCEDURE
1. Direct students to search the papers and magazines for examples of each of the literary terms and to paste their findings on the appropriate posters.

2. Leave completed posters on display so that students may become familiar with many examples of these literary terms.

3. At a subsequent time, give each student a copy of the "Literary Lingo" work sheet. Direct students to fill in each "poster" with as many original examples of each literary term as possible.

LITERARY LINGO

Make this miniature bulletin board come alive with your own original figures of speech and examples of literary terms.

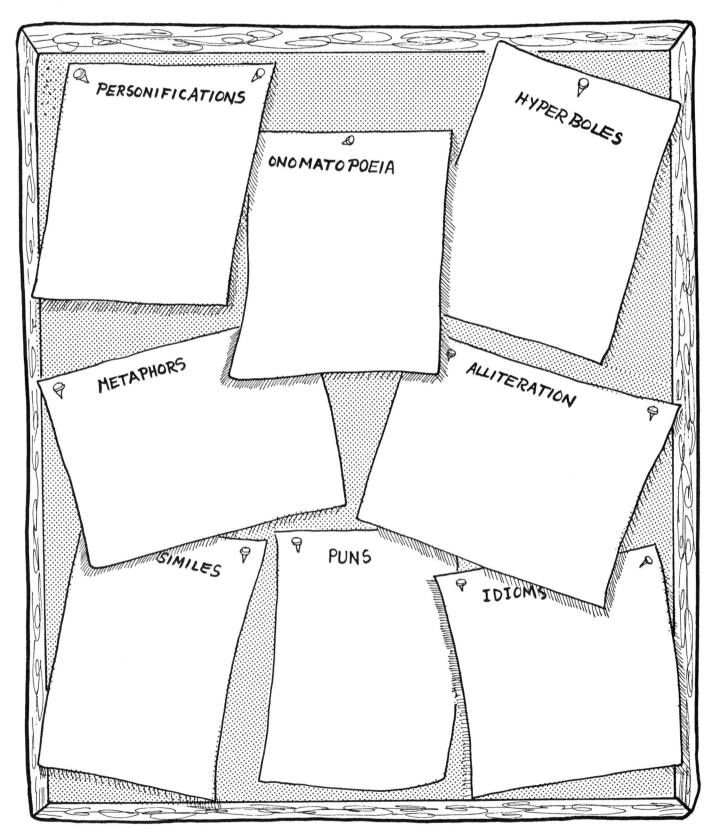

PURPOSE: Using sensory appeal

PREPARATION

1. Ask students to close their eyes and picture in their minds the most delicious foods they can imagine.

2. Then, ask them to think of words and phrases they might use to describe the foods. Write these on the chalkboard as they are suggested. Try to fill the entire board with words and phrases that have sensory appeal.

3. Provide a copy of the "Meal Appeal" work sheet for each student, along with various colors of construction paper, paste, scissors, and crayons.

PROCEDURE

1. Students color, cut out, and use the food pictures from the work sheet to create a "Meal Appeal" menu. Direct them to name and price the items, and to create a restaurant name to be used as the title for the menu.

2. Beside each picture, students must describe the item in terms that are so strong in sensory appeal that they make the reader's digestive juices begin to flow. (The words collected on the chalkboard may be used for reference.)

3. Collect the finished menus, and display them for all to enjoy.

WHO'S THE VILLAIN?

Has it ever occurred to you that the story of "The Three Little Pigs" might possibly make the big, bad wolf look like the villain when he really wasn't? Think about the poor old wolf who was teased and taunted, and finally murdered by the pigs. What about his side of the story?

Pretend that you are a newspaper reporter who got to talk to the wolf before he died. On the lines below, write an account of the story based on your interview with the wolf as a news story which appeared in the local paper the day after the wolf died. Don't forget your headline!

Village News

SATURDAY   MARCH 28, 1981   HALF PENCE

EGG-OMANIA

Egg-omania is "cracking" people up! They are putting one "over easy" on their friends!

See how many of the eggs you can "unscramble."

= _Exit_

"Eggs" + "Hit" = "Eggs-Hit" or, EXIT!

1. + SALT = _____

2. + SAM = _____

3. + = _____

4. + = _____

5. + = _____

6. + = _____

The sentences at the top of this page use puns. Look up the meaning of the word pun in the dictionary. Then use the space here to write a pun or two of your own!

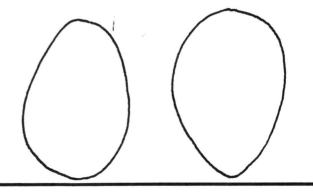

AD ANALYST

PURPOSE: Using emotional appeal

PREPARATION

1. Write the following four phrases on the chalkboard.

   —appeal to sentiment
   —appeal to desire for status or success
   —appeal to desire for adventure
   —appeal to sense of economy

2. Reproduce and provide a copy of the following page of advertising for each student.

3. Provide dictionaries for reference.

PROCEDURE

1. Make certain that students understand the meaning of each phrase on the board. They may use dictionaries to check the definitions if necessary.

2. Direct students to study the page of ads carefully to try to understand the intent or purpose of each one.

3. Students then write one or more of the four purposes on the line provided beneath each ad.

4. Students circle the key word or words in each ad that helped most in understanding the intent of the ad.

1.

2.

3.

4.

A PROBLEM OF PERSPECTIVE

A very well-known poet named Shel Silverstein created a poem in which he pretended he was writing from inside a lion. It changed the normal climate or position from which he would be writing.

Try writing a short mini-story from each of these unusual "climates."

. . . from inside a bottle . . .

. . . from inside a volcano . . .

. . . from atop the cherry on the world's largest hot fudge sundae . . .

. . . from underneath Big Foot's foot . . .

THAT BAG HAS ANOTHER USE

PURPOSE: Imagery

PREPARATION

1. Use brown paper bags with a single object inside each.

2. As an example, hold up one bag, take out the object and lead a class discussion centered on possible uses for the object. Encourage imaginative and unusual responses. List suggested uses on the board, and continue discussion in a fun but "no-nonsense" setting so long as spontaneous contributions are being offered.

3. Then ask the students to follow the directions below.

PROCEDURE

1. Select one bag each.

2. List as many uses for the object inside the bag as you can. S—T—R—E—T—C—H your mind for new and different ones.

3. At the end of ten minutes, the person with the longest list of uses for his/her object is declared the winner of the game, and gets to read his/her list to the group.

4. All lists could be placed in the bag with the proper object, bags arranged on a table and, for the next few days, students can enjoy looking at the objects and adding to the lists.

Just for Fun

How many uses can you think of for . . .
  Cinderella's coach
  a four-leaf clover
  your principal's desk

HYPERBOLE HYSTERIA

Hyper-what? Do you know how to pronounce that word? Do you know what it means? Haven't you been told at least a million times to look up words you don't know? Well, look it up. Mark its pronunciation and write its definition in the space below. Then, underline the hyperbole in this paragraph.

HYPERBOLE— _____

_____

See, all those million pieces of advice paid off!

Below are 32 phrases or sentences. Some of them are hyperboles; others are not. Circle the number of each hyperbole.

1. A rolling stone gathers no moss.
2. I'm so hungry I could eat a horse.
3. Well, I'll be a monkey's uncle!
4. His head's as big as a barrel.
5. I've told you a million times not to do that.
6. Haste makes waste.
7. Your suitcase weighs a ton!
8. One, two, buckle my shoe.
9. He could write his autobiography on the head of a pin.
10. That snake was a mile long.
11. My mind was going in a thousand different directions.
12. If that's so, I'll eat my hat.
13. That baby is as light as a feather.
14. Rise and shine!
15. My new jeans cost a fortune!
16. If I ate that much, I'd be as big as a house.
17. Early to bed, early to rise . . .
18. May I sew you to a sheet?
19. Oh, Mable, I haven't seen you for at least a hundred years!
20. Don't forget to write.
21. She moves slower than a glacier.
22. He talks ninety miles an hour.
23. It took me forever to read that book.
24. I'm going crazy!
25. He runs faster than a speeding bullet.
26. I could sleep for a year.
27. A penny saved is a penny earned.
28. She's as high as a kite.
29. You're a turkey.
30. A stitch in time saves nine.
31. Her hairdo is as old as Methuselah.
32. An apple a day keeps the doctor away.

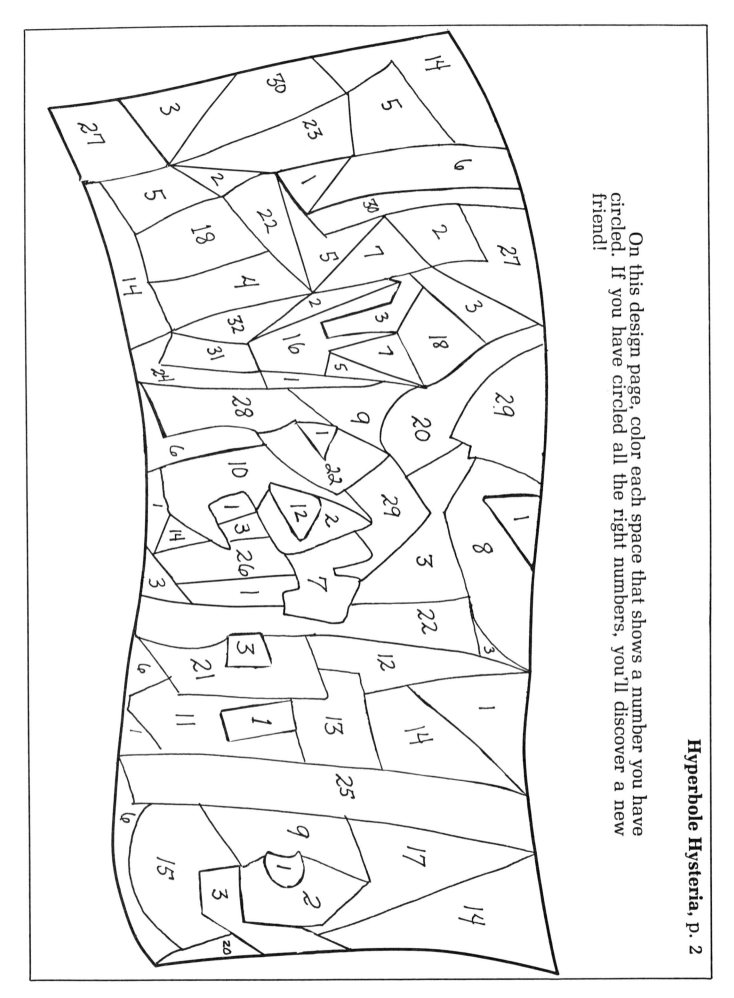

On this design page, color each space that shows a number you have circled. If you have circled all the right numbers, you'll discover a new friend!

Hyperbole Hysteria, p. 2

130

CAN YOU TELL A CHARACTER BY HIS COVER?

Carefully observe each of the three characters below. Think about what kind of person each might be. Now ask yourself what things about the character's appearance helped you decide what this person might be like.

In the circle beside each character, write a group of characteristics which describe that person. Then, in the box by each, write a paragraph describing something the person does that will demonstrate those characteristics.

DESCRIPTIONS BY DESIGN

Many companies mail catalogs by the thousands to customers all over the world. The descriptions given for the catalog items pictured are very important, since they may actually determine the customer's decision to order or not order an item.

On a separate sheet of paper, write brief paragraphs describing each of the items pictured below. Begin each paragraph with a catchy sentence to capture the reader's attention. Cut out the pictures, and paste them on the "Descriptions by Design" work sheet. Copy each of your descriptive paragraphs beside its corresponding picture to make a page for a toy catalog.

A.

A. _____

_____

_____

_____

_____

B.

B. _____

_____

_____

_____

_____

_____

_____

_____

_____

D.

D. _____

_____

_____

_____

_____

_____

_____

_____

C.

C. _____

_____

_____

_____

_____

E. _____

_____

_____

_____

_____

_____

_____

E.

F.

F. _____

_____

_____

_____

_____

_____

133

THE PRINCE'S DISCO BALL

THINGS ARE NOT WHAT THEY USED TO BE!

PURPOSE: Writing dialogue

PREPARATION

1. Acquire several books which include stories that can be dramatized. Mark the stories, or reproduce copies in sufficient quantites to meet group needs. (Old favorites such as "Three Billy Goats Gruff," "The Little Red Hen," "The Three Little Pigs," "Little Red Riding Hood," and "Goldilocks and the Three Bears" will work well.)

2. Provide a "good stuff junk box" full of old scarves, hats, paper bags, construction paper, scissors, paste, etc. Students can use these materials for prop and costume construction.

3. Divide students into small groups, and direct each group to select a story to be dramatized by following the Procedure directions.

PROCEDURE

1. Read and discuss the story selected.

2. Make a list of all the characters in the story.

3. Give the story a modern setting, and change the characters of the story accordingly.

4. Write the story in play form.

5. Use materials from the "good stuff junk box" to make costumes.

6. Stage your play as a TV Special, and present it for the rest of the class.

SILLY NILLY STORIES

PURPOSE: Writing a narrative story

PREPARATION

1. Provide lots of old magazines, scissors, paste, large sheets of construction paper, and pencils.

2. Prepare two or three "Silly Nilly" pictures to be used as starters (see directions on the following page).

3. Paste the "Write a Silly Nilly Story!" directions on a sheet of folded cardboard to make a study guide.

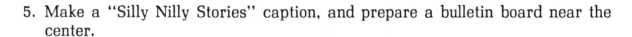

4. Place the materials in a free choice interest center.

5. Make a "Silly Nilly Stories" caption, and prepare a bulletin board near the center.

MAKE A Silly-Nilly

1. Make your own "Silly-Nilly" by cutting parts from two or three magazine pictures to put together to make one "crazy, couldn't be true!" illustration. Examples: a school bus full of children with the driver cut out and replaced by a hippopotamus; children on a picnic with one child replaced by a mermaid; an airplane in mid-air with its wings replaced by angel or butterfly wings.

2. Look through the magazine to find parts for your own "Silly Nilly". Compose your "Silly Nilly" carefully, and paste it on the top part of a sheet of construction paper.

3. Write a story to go with your "Silly Nilly." Think about your characters, and make up a plot to go with them. Try to give your story a dramatic or surprise ending.

4. Write your story on scratch paper first, and then copy it over carefully.

5. Add your story to the "Silly Nilly" bulletin board.

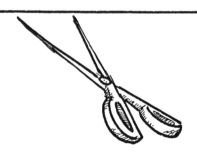

THE "BEAR" FACTS

News reporters know that their readers want the facts. They must report them without extra words or ideas, and without adding their own opinions about what happened.

Pretend that you were the reporter sent to investigate the story of "Goldilocks and the Three Bears," and gather the facts you need so that you can write the story. Use the Information File Card below to organize your facts. Then, in the lined space below, write the story as it might have appeared in the Bearville Banner.

REPORTER'S INFORMATION FILE CARD

What happened? –
    or
Who did something? –
When did it happen? –
Where did it happen? –
Why or How did it happen? –

BEARVILLE BANNER

TODAY'S NEWS AT YESTERDAY'S PRICE
5¢

The "Bear" Facts, p. 2

Read each of the following stories (find them in a library book or in your class library collection) to refresh your memory, and fill in the Information File Card on each one. (If you can't locate the stories, use what you do remember and create additional facts to supplement that, or make up stories of your own.)

A. "Paddington Bear"

A.

WHAT HAPPENED?
   OR
WHO DID SOMETHING?

WHEN DID IT HAPPEN?

WHERE DID IT HAPPEN?

WHY OR HOW DID IT HAPPEN?

B. "How the Bear Lost His Tail"

B.

WHAT HAPPENED?
   OR
WHO DID SOMETHING?

WHEN DID IT HAPPEN?

WHERE DID IT HAPPEN?

WHY OR HOW DID IT HAPPEN?

C.

WHAT HAPPENED?
   OR
WHO DID SOMETHING?

WHEN DID IT HAPPEN?

WHERE DID IT HAPPEN?

WHY OR HOW DID IT HAPPEN?

C. "Pooh Gets Into a Tight Place"

Choose one of the above. Use your Fact Card to write that news story on the back of this paper. Be prepared to share your story with the class.

RING AROUND the COUPLET

PURPOSE: Creating couplets

PREPARATION
1. Reproduce the game board on the following pages and paste inside a file folder or onto stiff paper.

2. Trace a quarter to make two circles. Leave one white, and shade the other to match the shaded circles on the game board. Paste these two circles to the two sides of a quarter.

3. Place the game board, the quarter, and some buttons of different colors (to be used as markers) where students may have free access to them.

PROCEDURE
1. Two students choose markers and place them on "Start."

2. The first student tosses the quarter and moves the marker to the nearest ring that matches the "up" side of the quarter.

3. The student must then create a couplet using the two rhyming words which appear in that ring.

4. If the student cannot create a couplet using the given words, he/she remains on that spot but forfeits the next turn.

5. After the first student finishes his/her turn, the second student tosses the quarter, moves accordingly, and tries to make a couplet.

6. The game continues in this manner until one player reaches the "Goal" to win the game.

START

DAY
STAY

MORE
SORE

HAIR
BEAR

GO
BLOW

CRY
FRY

CUP
UP

EIGHT
LATE

WOOD
STOOD

HAD
DAD

RHYME IN TIME

The rhythm of poetry makes it especially fun to say and hear. Often, the last words of the lines form a rhyming pattern.

Read these poems, and use matching colors to underline the lines that rhyme. Then, mark the lines that are the same color with the same letter.

The day I **tried**   A
To eat a whole *cake*   B
I nearly **died**   A
Of a stomach *ache!*   B

I beg you, please,   ____
Try not to sneeze.   ____
It makes a breeze,   ____
And spreads disease!   ____

Candy   ____
Is dandy!   ____
Stew . . .   ____
Phew!!   ____

Jack be nimble   ____
Jack be quick   ____
Jack jump over
The candlestick!

On a morning hung heavy with fog   ____
Quite early, I went for a jog.   ____
   Still mostly asleep,   ____
   I neglected to leap,   ____
And landed my head on a log!   ____

Little Bo Peep   ____
Has lost her sheep   ____
And can't tell where to find them.   ____
Leave them alone   ____
And they'll come home   ____
Wagging their tails behind them.   ____

Here's the Time . . . YOU Make the Rhyme!!

Write a rhyming poem on each of the line sets below. Make the rhyming lines in your poem match the rhyme patterns marked, and make one set of the rhyming words rhyme with the time shown on the nearest clock.

     Example:

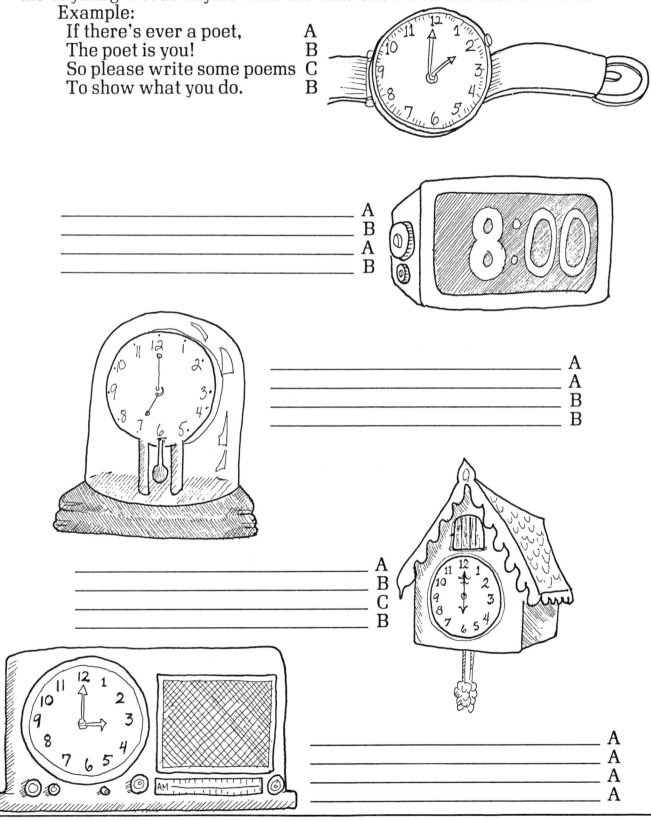

    If there's ever a poet,   A
    The poet is you!   B
    So please write some poems C
    To show what you do.   B

_____ A
_____ B
_____ A
_____ B

_____ A
_____ A
_____ B
_____ B

_____ A
_____ B
_____ C
_____ B

_____ A
_____ A
_____ A
_____ A

LOVIN' LIMERICKS

In a boggy old marsh by the sea ____

Sat a frog on a log lonesomely ____

There in his own shade ____

He spied a mermaid ____

And coaxed her to sit on his knee. ____

That is a lovin' limerick!

Do you know what makes a poem a limerick? First, it must have a special rhyme scheme. The first two lines rhyme with each other, the second two lines with each other, and the last line rhymes with the first two lines. This rhyme scheme is written a-a-b-b-a.

Label the rhyme scheme in the lovin' limerick above by writing in the correct letters in the correct spaces.

A limerick also has a special rhythm pattern.

Line 1 has 3 accented syllables.
Line 2 has 3 accented syllables.
Line 3 has 2 accented syllables.   Read the above limerick
Line 4 has 2 accented syllables.   aloud. Can you hear the
Line 5 has 3 accented syllables.   special rhythm pattern?

Use this space to write pairs or groups of rhyming words that could be used in writing lovin' limericks. A few are listed for you.

mine	love	marry	care	keep	heart
fine	dove	Harry	fair	leap	apart
Valentine	above	tarry	hair	weep	dart

merry	pair	you	tear	_____ _____
cherry	rare	blue	dear	_____ _____
very	stare	too	near	_____ _____

_____ _____ _____ _____
_____ _____ _____ _____
_____ _____ _____ _____

_____ _____ _____ _____
_____ _____ _____ _____

Use your groups of rhyming words to create a special limerick about each of these lovin' pairs.

A FRECKLE AND A HAIR

PEANUT BUTTER & JELLY

A BOY AND A TOAD

A BOOK AND A BOOKWORM

A SHOE AND A FOOT

PURPOSE: Writing haikus, cinquains, and free verse

PREPARATION
1. Bring apples, celery, carrots, or a combination of all three to the classroom—at least one for each student.

2. Provide a copy of the following pages for each student, a pencil, a sheet of writing paper, and an appropriate environment for a creative writing activity.

PROCEDURE
1. Each student chooses a piece of fruit or a vegetable.

2. The student then follows these instructions given by the teacher.

    1. Write three words that tell how your food looks.
    2. Write two words that describe its shape.
    3. Hold it in one hand, close your eyes, and rub it gently with the other hand. Write a word that describes its texture.
    4. Close your eyes again. Smell your food. Write two words that describe its fragrance.
    5. Take a bite. Write a sound word that describes what you heard when you bit it.
    6. Write two similes that tell how it feels in your mouth and on your tongue.
    7. Write three adjectives that describe its taste.
    8. Write a line that personifies the fruit or vegetable.
    9. Name a person or thing this object reminds you of, and tell why.
    10. If you could rename this fruit or vegetable, what appropriate name would you give it?

3. After following the instructions, the student uses that information to complete the three work sheets.

HAIKU HIBACHI

The Japanese invented a very beautiful form of poetry called haiku. It is unrhymed, has three lines, and refers in some way to one of the seasons of the year.

Your fruit or vegetable is a very special product of one of those seasons. Use this Japanese hibachi to "cook up" a haiku about your fruit or vegetable, and write it below. Don't forget to add a hint of the correct season.

Remember, in a haiku, line 1 must have five syllables; line 2 must have seven syllables, and line 3 must have five syllables.

147

ODE TO AN ORANGE

orange
tangy, sweet
sparkling, juicing, tempting
fragrant like spring blossoms
Sunshine!

This form of poetry is called cinquain. Its characteristic features are:
    Line 1—one word, a subject or an idea
    Line 2—two words, adjectives describing the subject
    Line 3—three words, verbs related to subject
    Line 4—four words, telling your reaction to subject
    Line 5—one word, a synonym for the subject

Take a special look at your fruit or vegetable. Reread the words you have collected during the first part of this activity. Then, pretending that your fruit or vegetable has some human qualities,

write a poetic tribute in cinquain form here to honor it.

write a humorous cinquain here about the same food.

VEGGIES IN THE VERNACULAR
(AND FRUITS, TOO!)

*Pineapples in the sky
Cherries jubilee riding high
Bananas Flambe in sunset colors
Whipped cream mountains
        with marmalade peaks
And a strawberry breeze . . .
        Fruit float!*

That's a free verse—poetry that has a certain flowing rhythm, but no regular pattern of rhyme. It's fun to write because it frees the poet to use language just as he/she wishes.

In each food shape below, write a short free verse poem that gives your own special impression about that food.

149

FUN WITH PHOETRY *

PURPOSE: Writing quatrains and
diamantes

PREPARATION
1. Review with the students the
   definitions and features of the
   quatrain and the diamante poetry
   forms.

   Quatrain—any four-line poem

   Example:

   A quatrain has poetic words
   Grouped in lines—just four.
   Fewer, not allowed at all . . .
   And never, never more!

*A combination of poetry and photographs

   Diamante—a seven line poem whose lines create a diamond shape.

Rules	Example
Line 1—one noun or pronoun	Diamante
Line 2—two adjectives	shaped, unusual
Line 3—three participles	exciting, entertaining, intriguing
Line 4—four nouns	thought, creation, harmony, description
Line 5—three participles	challenging, satisfying, lasting
Line 6—two adjectives	precise, brief
Line 7—one noun (usually a synonym for the first line)	Poem.

2. Provide magazines, paste, scissors, pens, and construction paper.

PROCEDURE
1. Each student looks through a magazine to find two photographs. He/she cuts out
   one in a rectangular or square shape and one in a diamond shape, and pastes
   these on light-colored construction paper.

2. The student creates a quatrain and writes it around the four edges of the
   square-cut photograph. Then, the student creates a diamante, writes it on a
   small, diamond-shaped piece of paper, and pastes it in the center of the diamond-
   shaped photo.

3. Students share and display their completed work.

PURPOSE: Writing titles

PREPARATION

1. Secure duplicate copies of magazines appropriate to the age and interest level of the students.

2. Cut out articles from one of the magazines. Remove the titles, and place each article in a separate envelope or manila folder.

3. Place the envelopes, pencils, paper, and the uncut magazine in a free choice interest center. Add a study guide giving the Procedure directions.

PROCEDURE

1. Select an envelope, and read the magazine article inside.

2. On a sheet of paper, write one to three sentences that give the main idea of the article.

3. Quickly skim the article again to make sure you have captured the main idea.

4. Write an interesting title for the article that you feel is representative of the main idea, and that would also encourage someone to read the article.

5. Now, check the title in the magazine to see how your title compares with the original.

BEAT THE PUBLISHER

PURPOSE: Writing titles, subtitles, and captions

PREPARATION
1. Find 2 copies of a specific issue of a newspaper or magazine.

2. Choose several articles from the publication, and cut them from each copy. Cut the articles apart at each place where a subtitle or caption appears. Then, clip off all titles, subtitles, and captions from the articles, and place the pieces in envelopes (one for each article). Attach each envelope to another envelope containing its matching, uncut article.

3. Give each student one or more envelope sets, a marking pen, white construction paper, and paste or tape.

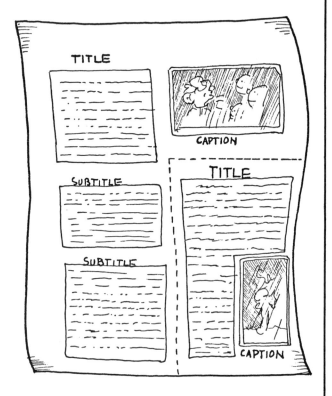

PROCEDURE
1. Each student takes the article pieces from the marked envelope and reads them carefully. He/she then orders the parts of the article and pastes them on the construction paper, leaving space between each article part.

2. The student then writes a title for the article and adds subtitles or captions (for pictures) in the spaces between each article part.

3. When the task is completed, the student may look in the other envelope to see the original title and subtitles for the article, and to compare those with his/her own. The student decides which he/she thinks is better, and writes a short paragraph telling what has been decided, and why.

The Incredible Proof Prince

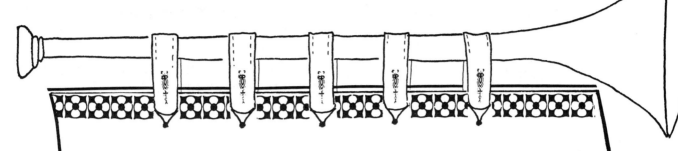

Once there was a Valiant prince who traveled the Kingdom of the Written Word making wrong things write he was called the Incredible Proof Prince because he made it his business to ferret our trouble here and there always leaving one of his special magic prints on an exact trouble spot causing it to turn out just write.

he was loved by every one in the Kingdom—everyone except the Duke of Error. The Duke was a rotten fellow who did what he could to cast evil spellings and cause mis understandings he even resorted to defacing distorting and destroying road signs so that travelers would become hopelessly lost and confused the Kingdom was miserable.

Finally, the incredible proof prince could stand it no longer he became enraged and shouted out out with Error! Nevermore shall you cause confusion in this kingdom! With that he drew his powerful proofreaders pen-sword and reduced the Duke of Error to an ordinary lower-case duke, no longer heralded by staunch exclamation points, but left hanging by freying threads to the coat tail of a cowardly question mark.

Long live the Incredible Proof Prince!!!

Unfortunately, the Proof Prince had to be out of the kingdom today.

Unfortunately, the Duke of Error has a young cousin who has created some trouble spots.

Fortunately, the prince has a friend like you who can use his magic prints to wipe out the troubles. Use the prince's proofreader's "prints" to correct the errors in the story.

THE WRITER'S BEST FRIEND

PURPOSE: Editing

PREPARATION

1. Locate a variety of newspaper and magazine articles which may be cut out and pasted on student work pages.

2. Provide at least two of the following kinds of articles for each student:

   1. a brief news, feature, or editorial item.
   2. a longer narrative magazine article.

3. Reproduce a copy of the following "Editor's Guide" for each student.

4. Discuss the role of the editor—one who critiques a piece of writing. Talk about the kinds of things an editor thinks about or looks for. Make the point that a writer's best friend is the editor, even though the editor may also be the writer's harshest critic, because he helps to make the finished product better. Also point out that self-editing is one of the best things a writer can learn to do.

5. Present the "Editor's Guide," and discuss the questions so that students will know how to use the guide effectively.

PROCEDURE

1. Distribute news and magazine articles to the students. Direct them to attach them to sheets of notebook paper.

2. Students then use the "Editor's Guide" as a guide for "editing" the articles and sharpening their own technical writing skills.

EDITOR'S GUIDE

Who wrote this article? _____

Who was his/her intended audience? _____

Do you think the piece appeals to that audience? _____

What response does the writer hope for? _____
_____

In your opinion, has the writer included enough information and presented
   his/her idea well enough to get that response? _____ Explain. _____
_____

Did the first few sentences attract your attention? _____

Was the writer's message easy to follow and understand? _____

Does the article end with a feeling or idea that leaves the reader with something to think about or make the reader glad that he/she has spent time
   reading the piece? _____

Has the writer used clear, accurate, easily understood words? _____

Underline the words or phrases in the article that could have been left out
   without changing any meanings.

Circle any overworked words or phrases.

Count the number of sentences that begin with "There" or "It." Rewrite one
   of the sentences here. _____
_____

Find the longest or most complicated sentence in the article. Rewrite the
   same thought here in shorter sentences. _____
_____
_____
_____

Did you like the writer's style? _____

Would you have chosen to read this article even if your teacher had not
   required it? _____ Why or why not? _____
_____
_____

These are some of the kinds of questions a good writer asks himself
when he edits his own writing.

On the back of this paper, write an article of 10-12 sentences about one
of the following statements. Then, edit it yourself, using these same questions.

Let a friend read and re-edit the article.

   —The next President should be a woman.
   —There ought to be a law against parents bossing children.
   —School should be in session all 12 months of the year, with one
     week off each month.
   —There should be no recognition in public schools of holidays
     celebrated by cultural, ethnic, or religious groups.
   —The sale of any candy which contains refined sugar should be
     outlawed.

COMPOSITION AND ORIGINAL WRITING
COMPETENCY REVIEW

1. Draw a line through the resource that would be least helpful in creating a map of a city.

   surveyor's reports
   biographies of people who live there
   outdated maps of the city

2. Circle the resource that would be the most helpful in writing a character description of the town mayor.

   interviews with the mayor's friends and neighbors
   the mayor's birth certificate
   a picture of the mayor's house

3. Number the sentences below in sensible, sequential order.

   __ A cat walked by and sniffed.
   __ A dead mouse lay on the street undisturbed.
   __ He crossed the street and prowled on.

4. Circle the letter by the example that shows a summary.

   A. 6:20—subject walks to car.
      6:29—subject arrives at office building.
      6:32—subject enters office of Attorney John Endine.
      7:14—subject leaves office.
      7:25—subject arrives at home.

   B. Subject makes a brief trip to attorney's office and returns home.

5. Draw a line through the pair that does not illustrate a paraphrase.

   Please do that quickly./Hurry.
   I can't hear you./Dumb.
   Put it down now./Drop it!

6. Circle the example of précis writing.

   There is a beautiful antique clock for sale which was crafted by Swiss experts. It has a china face encased in crystal and inlaid with gold. It also has a lovely chime which is as beautiful as any in the whole world.

   Antique Swiss clock for sale —China face, crystal case, gold inlay, fine chimes.

7. Write the letter of the literary term in the blank beside its example.

   A. Metaphor
   B. Simile
   C. Personification
   D. Alliteration
   E. Onomatopoeia

   __ She's as good as gold.
   __ Whoosh! Sloosh! Shush!
   __ He is a sly fox.
   __ She sells sea shells.
   __ Winter blows his cold breath across the land.

8. Identify the following forms of writing by placing the letter before each next to its example.

    A. Characterization
    B. News Report
    C. Dialogue
    D. Narrative
    E. Editorial
    F. Description

__ A bleak, wintry sky was the backdrop for a jovial meeting of six friendly government officials.

__ Mayor Charles Hager committed near political suicide today when he responded too hastily . . .

__ Spry and alert, ever optimistic, the mayor meets every challenge with a twinkle in his eye.

__ Mayor Charles Hager greeted officials from 5 neighboring cities today at 2:00 p.m. on the City Hall steps.

__ "Gentlemen, I am happy to see you," said the Mayor. "And we are very happy to be here," replied the visitors.

__ The story of how the lives of 6 important men became entwined in a common adventure is a long and exciting one. It all began back in 1894 when . . .

9. Circle the pair of lines that is a rhyming couplet.

Little Boy Blue,
Where are you?

Little Boy Blue,
Come blow your horn.

10. Circle the correct number of lines for a cinquain.
    5   4   3

11. Draw a line to match each poetic form with its appropriate rhyme scheme.

    limerick   AABBA
    couplets   none
    free verse   AABB

12. Place the correct mark by each item below.

    T—title
    C—caption
    L—label

    __ Dean's Strawberry Jam
    __ The Tale of Benjamin
    __ Wash out!

13. Be a good proofreader, and find five errors in this sentence. Put a circle around each error you find.

Yesterday Greg and Tina was on their way to buy lettuce, celery, and carrots when they run into Mrs Wilson.

SKILLS STUFF

Writing For Everyday Living

LETTER WRITING

____ Friendly, Social Notes, Business

____ Envelopes

INFORMATIONAL AND INSTRUCTIONAL WRITING

____ Graphs and Diagrams

____ Signs and Posters

____ Pictorial Directions

____ Procedural Directions

____ Geographical Directions

COMPLETING INFORMATIONAL FORMS

____ Identification and Registration

____ Applications

____ Contracts

____ Order Blanks

ORGANIZING AND RECORDING FACTUAL DATA

____ Record Keeping and Inventories

____ Memos

____ Biographies

____ Bibliographies

____ Checks and Deposits

____ Journals and Diaries

____ Lists

____ Ads

____ Reports

SOMETHING'S MISSING

In each of the letters below, the writer has left out a very important sentence. Read the letters, and write the missing sentences on the lines below.

Dear Grandma,

The book you sent for my birthday came yesterday. The mailman blew his whistle at the front door when he brought it.

Ten people came to my party. It was real cool, especially when I blew out the candles on my cake.

Love,
Joey

_____

_____

Dear Mom,

Camp is nice. I'm glad I came, even though I was a little homesick at first.

We are having a program for parents. We will have dances, a puppet play, and music. I know you will want to come, so just don't be late.

Your son,
Mike

_____

_____

A READY RESPONSE

Select one of the two letters from **"Something's Missing,"** and answer it as if you were the receiver.

Don't forget to include the five important parts of a good letter, and to use the correct punctuation marks.

Design a special stamp for your envelope.

THE SOCIAL SET

A social note may be formal or informal, and as long or as short as the sender wants it to be. The important thing about a social note is that it must carry the intended message.

Write a social note for each of the situations below.

an invititation to your birthday party

a "just to keep in touch" note to someone in another town

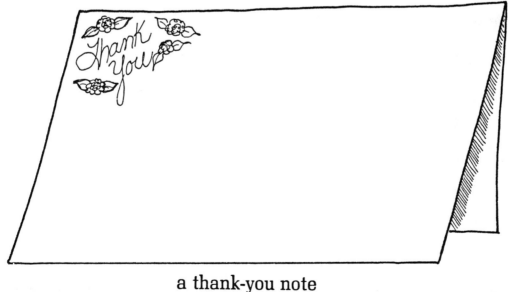

a thank-you note

INFORMATION REQUESTED

Julie Jacobsky lives at 913 West Iris Lane in Chicago, Illinois 60602. She wrote a letter to the Heartland Art Company, 919 Marymount Avenue, in St. Paul, Minnesota 55116, to request a catalog and to ask how long it should take for a shipment from the company to reach her.

Write Julie's letter in the space below. Use today's date.

RETURN TO SENDER

Julie addressed an envelope for her letter like this:

Her mother looked at the envelope and said that it would never be delivered. She reminded Julie that the Heartland Art Company in St. Paul, Minnesota, was located at 919 Marymount Avenue, and the ZIP Code was 55116.

Readdress her envelope correctly. (Don't forget capital letters and punctuation.)

TEMPERATURE TAKEOVER

PURPOSE: Practicing pictorial writing/graphs

PREPARATION

1. Prepare a large chart or bulletin board using the expected temperature range for your vicinity for five school days. Attach yarn and pins as shown.

2. Provide a weather thermometer, and place it near the chart.

3. Reproduce the "Temperature Takover" work sheet for the participants.

PROCEDURE

1. Lead a class discussion related to the temperature.

2. At the same time each day, read the thermometer, and attach the yarn to show the correct temperature.

3. Culminate the study on Friday by distrubuting copies of the work sheet. Direct students to show the temperature for the five days by using the marked chart to fill in the graph, and to complete the rest of the work sheet.

TEMPERATURE TAKEOVER WORK SHEET

Fill in the graph to show the temperature for the past five days.

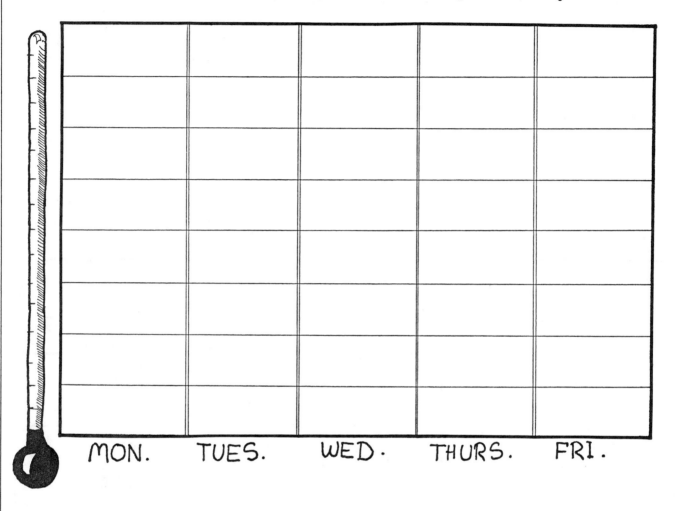

| MON. | TUES. | WED. | THURS. | FRI. |

Which day of the week was coolest?_____

Which day of the week had the highest temperature? _____

What is the average temperature for the past five days?_____

How many days did it rain? _____

What was the weather like when you got out of school on Wednesday?

_____

Write one sentence to describe the weather for the past five days.

_____

DIRECTIONS TO FOLLOW

Look at the diagram carefully. Write directions in each of the boxes on the "Directions to Follow" work sheet. Write your directions clearly and completely so that they could easily be followed without the diagram.

1.

2.

3.

4.

5.

6.

7.

8.

9.

1.

2.

3.

4.

5.

6.

7.

8.

9.

NO WORD WASTING ALLOWED!

Sometimes it is important to be able to write messages in the fewest words possible.

Read each of the messages below. Then, draw a sign, and use no more than three words in each to convey the meaning of each written message.

Example: You can reach the airport by going one mile straight down this road.

This wall has just been painted.

All cars must come to a complete stop at this intersection.

The exit for Interstate 65 is only one mile from here.

This parking space is to be used by handicapped persons only.

In case of fire, people are to leave the theater through this rear door.

Hamburgers are for sale here. They cost one dollar.

Drivers are requested to drive slowly and carefully through these three blocks because of the school.

NO WORD WASTING ALLOWED!

Write each message in a complete sentence beside its sign.

PURPOSE: Writing sign messages

PREPARATION

1. Lead a discussion of the value of road signs. Ask what would happen if all the road signs in the world suddenly disappeared.

2. Review the messages conveyed by the signs on the "No Word Wasting Allowed!" work sheet and other well-known road signs.

3. Supply newspapers, magazines, travel brochures, scissors, drawing paper, paste, crayons, and pencils. Place these materials, along with the Procedure directions, in a free choice interest center, or give the directions orally as a follow-up activity for the class discussion.

PROCEDURE

1. Select a magazine picture showing several signs, or a picture without signs to which signs could be added (a highway, city street, airport, housing development, etc.).

2. Cut out the picture, and paste it at the top of a piece of drawing paper.

3. Give the signs in the scene new meanings by supplying different words, and/or add more signs to give the scene an entirely new "feel."

4. Write a story about the picture with the new signs.

POST A THOUGHT

Posters are often designed to influence people's beliefs, values, or behavior.

Design a poster to influence other people to do one of the following things:

1. use the public library,
2. conserve natural resources,
3. play baseball,
4. save money,
5. be more polite,
6. vote in the next city election,
7. learn to swim.

Make up a catchy, one-line caption or a short poem or jingle. Use it with a clever, attractive illustration to carry your message.

CHAIN GANG

Paper chains are fun to make, especially for holiday or birthday party decorations.

Select a kind of chain you'd like to make. Gather the necessary art supplies, and make a chain that is your very own in color, shape, size, kind of paper, length, etc.

When your chain is complete, look at it carefully, and draw pictures to show someone who neither reads or speaks English how to make the chain. Remember, you will have to picture the supplies and every step in your construction.

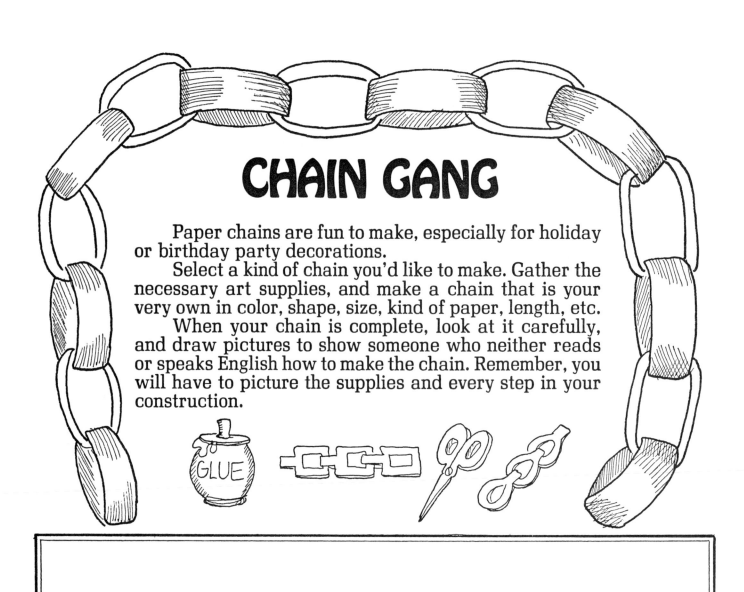

CRAFTY DIRECTIONS

Mary Mix-up is in a mess again. Saturday is the day of the long-awaited craft fair, and Mary is working frantically to get her entry ready. Since she is a creative person who likes to work with her hands, the bird feeder she plans to enter has been done for days. It is well made and looks lovely. Mary Mix-up's problem is one of organization. She is having problems writing the step-by-step direction card that is required. Help her put the jumbled-up steps in order and complete the card.

Mary's notes:

You make a string loop to hang the bird feeder from a tree branch after you have used a scissors to cut out a square opening in two sides of the milk carton. You punch holes in the sides of the carton, and run a small tree branch through the opening for the bird to perch on. The last thing you do is put in some bird seed. I painted the whole thing with blue tempera paint just to make it look pretty. I used my water colors to paint some bugs and flowers around the opening.

Materials:

_____

_____

_____

_____

_____

Directions:

_____

_____

_____

_____

_____

_____

_____

_____

_____

_____

Getting There!

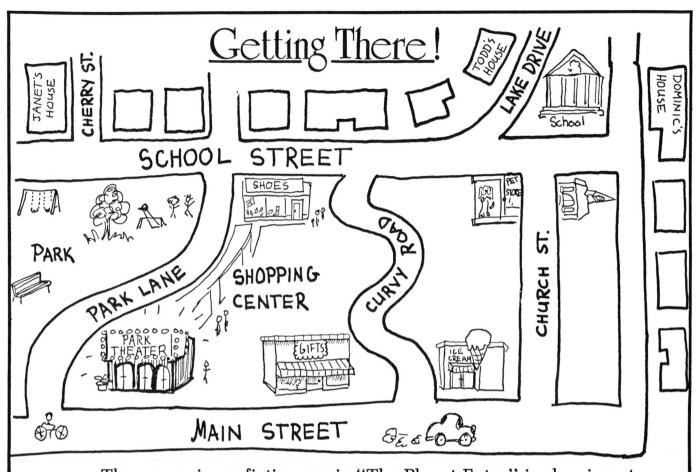

The new science-fiction movie "The Planet Eater" is showing at the Park Theater in the Main Street Shopping Center. Dominic, Todd and Janet plan to meet at the theater Saturday afternoon to see it, but none of them is sure just where the building is.

Read the map shown here. Then help the three friends get to the movie by making each of them a set of written directions from home to the theater.

JANET

TODD

DOMINIC

DIRECTION CORRECTION

Use the Shopping Center Directory to find answers to the questions following each situation.

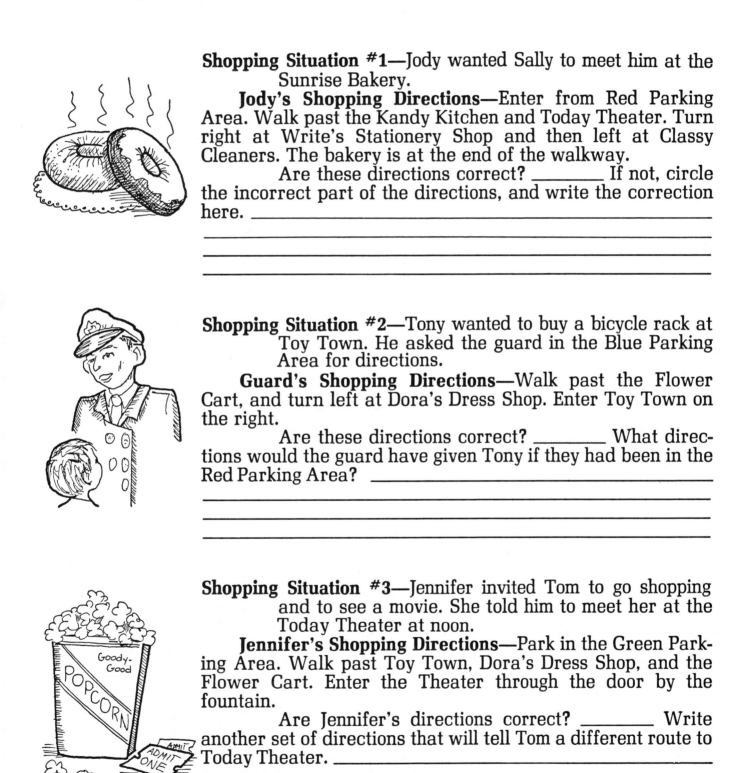

Shopping Situation #1—Jody wanted Sally to meet him at the Sunrise Bakery.

Jody's Shopping Directions—Enter from Red Parking Area. Walk past the Kandy Kitchen and Today Theater. Turn right at Write's Stationery Shop and then left at Classy Cleaners. The bakery is at the end of the walkway.

Are these directions correct? _____ If not, circle the incorrect part of the directions, and write the correction here. _____

_____

_____

_____

Shopping Situation #2—Tony wanted to buy a bicycle rack at Toy Town. He asked the guard in the Blue Parking Area for directions.

Guard's Shopping Directions—Walk past the Flower Cart, and turn left at Dora's Dress Shop. Enter Toy Town on the right.

Are these directions correct? _____ What directions would the guard have given Tony if they had been in the Red Parking Area? _____

_____

_____

_____

Shopping Situation #3—Jennifer invited Tom to go shopping and to see a movie. She told him to meet her at the Today Theater at noon.

Jennifer's Shopping Directions—Park in the Green Parking Area. Walk past Toy Town, Dora's Dress Shop, and the Flower Cart. Enter the Theater through the door by the fountain.

Are Jennifer's directions correct? _____ Write another set of directions that will tell Tom a different route to Today Theater. _____

_____

_____

_____

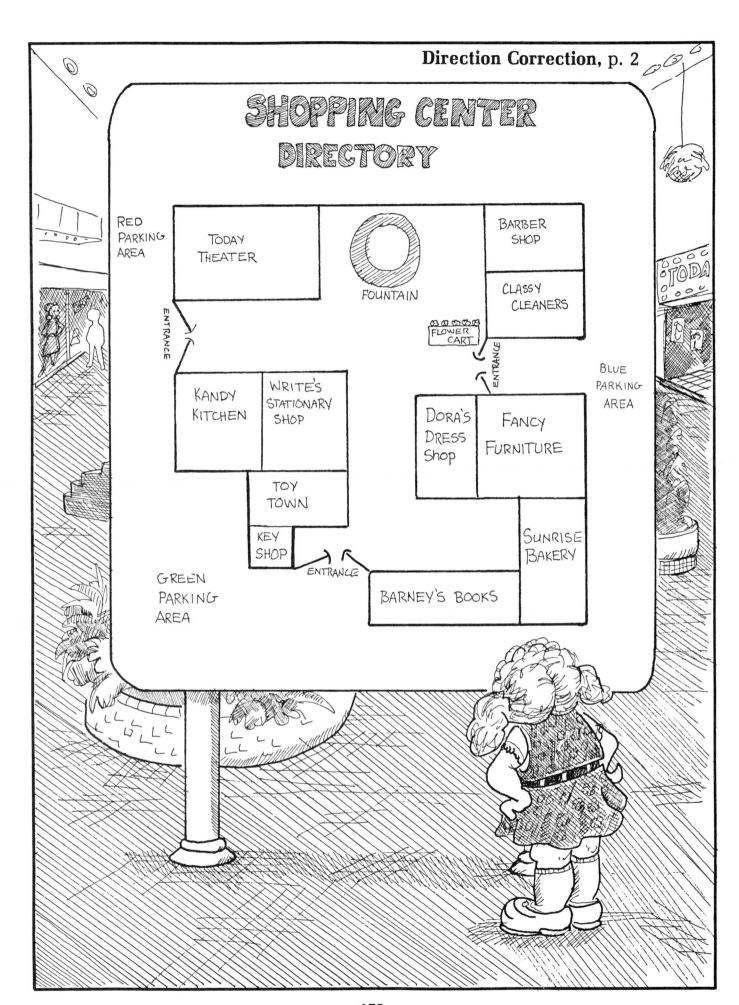

MAPS MAKE IT EASIER

Draw a map for each of the shopping situations in the "Direction Correction" activity.

Situation #1

Situation #2

Situation #3

OFFICIAL INFORMATION

Complete this "Official Information Form" as if you were your own parent or guardian.

Pupil Information Form

Pupil's Name _____
(Last)   (First)   (Middle)

Date of Birth: Month_____ Day_____ Year_____ Sex: M_____ F_____

Birth Certificate Number (1st Grade Pupils Only):_____

Name of Parent or Guardian _____ Phone _____

Address _____
(Street)   (Subdivision)   (Route)

With whom is child now living? _____ Relationship_____

Full Name, Place of Employment, and Job for:

Father_____

Mother _____

Father's Work Phone _____ Mother's Work Phone _____

Family Physician _____ Phone _____

How many years has the child   General health conditions: _____
attended school? _____   _____

Does child have any seeing, hearing, or speech problems? _____

If so, explain. _____

How many children are in your family? _____ Names and grades of

sisters and brothers in this school: _____

_____

Signature of parent or guardian _____ Date _____

MORE OFFICIAL INFORMATION

Complete this data card for the principal's file.

Last Name	First	Middle	Grade	Birthday	Locker #	Home Room Teacher

M F   W B Other

Sex ___ ___ Race ___ ___ _____

Parents _____

Phone _____ Emerg. # _____

Address _____

Occupation of Parents:

    Father _____

    Mother _____

Family Doctor _____

Other _____

Subject	Period	Teacher
	1	
	2	
	3	
	4	
	5	
	6	
	7	

School Year _____

Dropped _____
                    (Date)

Reason_____

Records _____

Complete this request for a library card.

Library Card Request

Name _____

Parents' Names_____

Address _____

Phone _____ Age _____

School _____ Grade _____

Date _____ Signature_____

List three other information forms you have filled out.

1. _____ 2. _____ 3. _____

JOB WANTED

Select a summer job from the Want Ads below that you feel would be interesting to you.

Write a letter applying for the job. Remember, applications should be brief and to the point. Give your qualifications in five sentences or less.

Kids Needed! to pull weeds & cut grass. 9 to 3, 5 days/week. $2.00 per hour. Apply to B. Bascalupo. Public Parks, Dept. 6F, Freeport, FL 33289

Boy to deliver packages. Bicycle a must. 9 to 5, Mon. through Sat. Good pay! Apply by letter to J. Swingbottom, Handy's Dept. Store, Public Square, Cold Springs, VT 01089

Dishwashers! Petro's Diner, 604 N. Main St., Sunnyvale, MI 48009. Evelyn Scruggs, Mgr. Hours flexible, 5 hours per day, $12.50. No experience required.

Young people needed to work with 4-yr.-old kids at Betty Boope Day Care Ctr. 4 hours/day, either A.M. or P.M. Salary set by qualifications. Ms. Jo James, Dir., 604 Ivey St., St. Thomas, RI 00342

Dependable & considerate boy or girl to run errands & be summer companion for elderly man. 10 to 2, 6 days a week. Lovely home: lunch furnished. $50 per week. Write Mr. T. S. Jamison, 604 Commerce St., Waco, TX 77067

Ambitious girl needed to assist beautician at Barbara's Beauty Box, 7011 Lucky Blvd., Main Chance, MD 06435

JOB OF THE MOMENT

Iva Moment lives with her parents, Mr. and Mrs. Justa Moment, at ninety-nine hundred River Road in St. Thomas, Rhode Island. Her Zip Code is 00342, and her phone number is 934-4670. She is twelve years old, a brunette with blue eyes, weighs seventy-six pounds, and is four feet, three inches tall. She has just finished the sixth grade at St. Andrew's School, and is a straight A student, except for physical education. Since she likes to read a lot and is not especially interested in sports or games, she does not do well in this area.

Last summer, she worked as a clean-up girl two days a week at Barbara's Beauty Box. During the school year, she babysat for the Jones children next door for 95¢ an hour. This summer, she has secured her parents' permission to apply for a few jobs in her own neighborhood. She is especially interested in the day care position because she likes kids and thinks she would be a good teacher's helper.

Fill out this application for her.

Classified advertisement (clipping):

Hours flexible, 5 hou— per day, $16.00. No experience required. Young people needed to work with 4-yr.-old kids at Betty Boope Day Care Ctr. 4 hours/day, either A.M. or P.M. Salary set by qualifications. Ms. Jo James, Dir., 604 Ivey St., St. Thomas, RI 00342

Betty Boope Day Care Center
Application for Employment

Name _____ Phone _____

Address_____

Age _____ Weight _____ Height _____

Job applied for _____

Education _____

Special talents that qualify you for this position _____

_____

_____

Past experience _____

_____

Salary expected _____

References: Person   Address

_____

_____

Give a three sentence statement telling why you want this job.

_____

_____

_____

Lucky Iva Moment got the job! She'll be working from two until six, five days a week, for the rest of the summer. When she reported for work, Mrs. Jo James asked her to fill out an information form so that her idenfication card could be issued.

Using Iva's personal data from the "Job of the Moment" activity, complete this form.

IDENTIFICATION SHEET

Name _____

            (Last)   (First)   (Middle)

Residence _____

Zip Code _____ Phone _____

Person to be notified in case of emergency:

_____

            (Last)   (First)   (Middle)

Address _____ Phone _____

Personal Physician _____ Phone _____

Age _____ Weight _____ Height _____

Color of eyes _____ Color of hair _____

School _____

Last grade completed _____

CAREER MINDED

(A Study Project Contract for Exploring a Career)

My Name _____

Career to be explored _____

I chose this career because _____

_____

Books and periodicals I will read_____

_____

Other sources of information I will use _____

_____

Field trips, resource people, and other activities _____

_____

_____

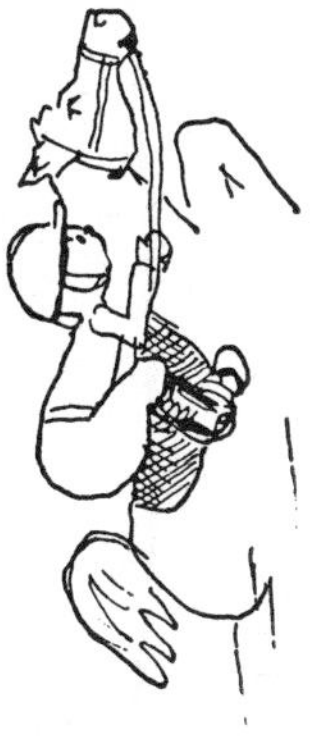

My project will be completed by _____

I will present my project to the class on _____

I will present my project to the class by:

show and tell ____   handouts ____
lecture ____   other _____
notebook ____   _____

I will have a conference with the teacher on_____

I would like my project evaluated in the following way:

_____

Signature _____

Teacher's Signature _____ Date _____

THIS SCHOOL YEAR IS IN THE BAG

This is an order blank from a catalog your teacher might use to order materials for your classroom. Look around your room, and take inventory of the materials and supplies on hand. Think of the kinds of things you like to do and the materials needed to do them. From the listings in the bags on the following page, make out an order that you would like your teacher to send. Use your teacher's name and school address on the order form.

The BCD Company
9432 General Philpot Dr.
Morningside, MT 56803
Phone: 924-4612 (406)

Order Blank
BCD-98

Please Print or Type

Ship To: Name_____
School _____
Address _____
City/State/Zip _____
Phone # _____

Quantity (State by unit of sale: Each; Pkg; etc. as in catalog.)	Product	Price per Catalog Unit	Extension (total)

Shipping charges vary greatly depending on type and weight of merchandise. Please include 10% of the merchandise value for shipping.

Merchandise Total	
Shipping Charges	
Total	

Please pay **FULL** amount due.

This School Year... is in The Bag!

MATH

MATH-O-MAGIC GAMES	6.00
MATH WORKBOOK	3.00
GIANT MATH QUIZ BOOK	9.00
MATH SKILLS SHEETS	6.00
HARD MATH	8.00
EASY MATH	8.00

ART SUPPLIES

MAGIC CRAYONS .... Box of 24	3.50
SUPER CLAY .... 3 lb. Box	5.00
FELT TIP PENS .... 1 DOZ	6.50
POSTER PAINT .... CARTON	5.00
TAG BOARD .... per sheet	1.00
DRAWING PAPER .... 1 PKG	2.50
POSTER PAPER .... 1 PKG	3.00
TISSUE PAPER .... 1 PKG	3.50
GLUE .... 1 DOZ	12.00

READING, SPELLING

READING WORKBOOK	3.50
READING GAMEBOOK	7.50
CROSSWORD PUZZLE BOOK	5.50
SPELLING WORKSHEETS (1 PKG)	4.00
POETRY PICKINGS BOOK	6.50
GUIDE TO THE LIBRARY	3.90

WRITING

LINED PAPER .... pkg	6.00
HANDWRITING GUIDE	7.00
STORY STARTER BOOK	5.50
DICTIONARY	9.00

SCIENCE

TEST TUBES .... PKG	5.00
MICROSCOPE	100.00
WONDERS OF SCIENCE BOOK	6.50
SCIENCE GAMEBOOK	5.00

PHYS ED AND MUSIC

BASEBALL, GLOVE, HAT	24.00
JUMP ROPE	3.00
GAME BOOK	6.00
VOLLEYBALL AND NET	12.00
MELODY RECORD	6.50
RHYTHM BAND INSTRUMENTS	27.00

GOODIES

CHALK (PASTEL) pkg	1.90
MULTI-COLORED YARN pkg	2.00
WALL CALENDAR	5.00
GAME ASSORTMENT 4 per pkg	10.00

HOW WELL DO YOU EAT?

Many people today are becoming more concerned about eating the right foods to build strong, healthy bodies. One of the first steps toward establishing good eating habits is to find out what really is being eaten.

Use this form to keep a record of all the food you eat this week.

	BREAKFAST 	LUNCH 	DINNER 
SUN.			
MON.			
TUES.			
WED.			
THURS.			
FRI.			
SAT.			

At the end of the week, circle all of the "healthy" meals that you ate, and draw a line through the "junk food" meals.

Compare the two. How healthy are your eating habits?

_____

_____

READING LOG

Name _____

Week of _____ Goal (Number of books) _____

Date	What I'm Reading	Pages	What It's About	New or Difficult Words

PERSONAL PROPERTY

An inventory is a listing of current assets. You may be surprised to realize what goods you have on hand at this very minute that make up your assets.

Check your desk, your pockets, purse, lunch box, locker, and any other place you may have property that belongs to you **at school** right now. List it all, and feel rich!

Inventory of Personal Property Belonging to:

_____ on _____
(Name)   (Date)

_____

_____

_____

_____

_____

_____

_____

_____

_____

_____

_____

_____

_____

List the three most valuable items on your inventory sheet.

1._____

2._____

3._____

Which is the most useful? _____

MINI MESSAGES

Memo is short for memorandum. A memo is a very short message written to give some very specific information in the fewest words possible.

Write a memo for each of the messages below. Remember, use the fewest words possible, but make sure your memo tells what, when, where, and why.

The cookie chairman of Girl Scout Troop 92 needs to tell all scouts in the troop that cookies are to go on sale Tuesday, May 14. The cookies are to be picked up at her house, 114 Glendale St., between 2 and 4 p.m. next Saturday.

The chief of the Fire Department needs to call a meeting of all volunteer firemen on Friday, July 13, at 3:30 in the afternoon at the main firehall.

The principal of your school wants to tell all teachers in the school that the halls are too noisy, and that he wants fewer students in the main hall between classes. He also wants to remind teachers of the "no talking in the lunch room" policy.

Write a memo on a separate sheet of paper to tell your teacher something you really think he or she should know.

191

ANATOMY OF A BIOGRAPHY

PURPOSE: Collecting and organizing factual data.

PREPARATION
1. Reproduce the "Biographical Data Work Sheet."

PROCEDURE
1. Discuss the elements of a good biography and, if necessary, give examples by displaying biographies of famous people well known to the students.

2. Pair students to write each other's biography.

3. Distribute copies of the "Biographical Data Work Sheet."

4. Direct students to:
    1. interview the person whose biography they are to write,
    2. complete the data sheet,
    3. then write the biography, and include the author's name.

5. Collect completed biographies, and hold them for use in the "Publisher's Listing" activity.

BIOGRAPHICAL DATA WORK SHEET

Name _____

Parents' Names _____

Address _____

Date of Birth _____ Time _____

Place _____

Weight and Length at Birth_____

Favorite Things (sport, toy, song, TV program, foods) _____

_____

_____

Names and Ages of Brothers and/or Sisters _____

_____

_____

Special Talents _____

_____

Life Ambitions or Goals _____

_____

Three Wishes _____

_____

Other Items of Importance _____

_____

_____

PURPOSE: Writing a bibliography/proofreading

PREPARATION

1. Assemble construction paper, felt pens, and staplers for the students. Glue the Study Guide on the following page to a piece of tag board.

2. Place all materials in a learning center setting (or vary instructions and use as a directed teaching or home work activity).

PROCEDURE

1. Lead a class discussion related to publishing original writing. Display copies of two or three books of interest to the students, calling attention to the copyright page.

2. To acquaint students with bibliographic form, ask each to take a book from his/her desk, turn to the copyright page, and make a bibliographic listing for the book. (You may need to write one on the chalkboard for reference.)

   Example: Forte, Imogene. *Skillstuff-Reading.* Nashville:
   Incentive Publications, Inc., 1979.

3. Use your grade or room number as a publishing company name (example: Fourth Grade Publications), and direct students to complete the learning center tasks in their free time.

4. Elect a committee to make a bibliography of all the biographies completed in the "Anatomy of a Biography" activity. Also elect a proofreading committee.

5. Review procedures for proofreading with the entire group. (See the Yellow Pages of this book for Proofreaders' Marks, and use that as a guide for making a set for your bulletin board.)

6. Place the proofed and corrected bibliography and all completed biographies in the learning center. Provide time, and encourage all students to use the bibliography to select at least three or four biographies to read.

PUBLISHER'S LISTING STUDY GUIDE

1. Reread the biography you have just completed. Correct any errors in spelling or punctuation.

2. Give your biography a "catchy" name.

3. Select a color of paper, and use felt pens to design a cover. Make your cover as attractive as possible to encourage people to read your book.

4. Make a title page and a copyright page for your book.

5. Staple your book together.

6. Complete a bibliography card for your book. Remember to give the following information, and to use the correct punctuation.

Author's last name	First name
Title of Book	
Publisher	
Place of publication	Date

7. An annotated bibliography contains a very brief description of each book. Write a two- or three- sentence annotation for your book on your bibliography card.

CHECK-UP

Heidi Harrison is a well-organized young lady who works hard and plans how to spend her money wisely. She has just opened her first checking account, and is being very careful to live up to this new responsibility.

The banker reminded Heidi that a check is a written order telling the bank to take the sum of money specified from the account of the person who has signed the check. The banker also reminded Heidi to always remember to include:

1. the date,
2. the name of the person to receive the money,
3. the exact amount,
4. the signature.

Help Heidi by completing these checks. Use the months and days given, but add this year's date.

She purchased a pair of sunglasses from the Seeing Person Co. for $9.75 on March 3rd.

Heidi wrote a check for $5.00 to her little sister, Renee Harrison, on her birthday, July 6th.

The National Nature Museum dues were due on July 19th. Heidi wrote a check that day for her $6.00 annual dues.

On the first day of school, Heidi bought a notebook, three pencils, a pen, and a book bag from the Pierce School Book Store. She wrote a check for $9.22 for her purchase on August 27th.

BANKING BUSINESS

Banking *is* serious business. Writing checks and keeping a checkbook in balance takes a little extra thought and effort at first, but it is a good way to keep a record of where and how you spend your money.

Use this page from Heidi Harrison's checkbook. Add the following deposits to practice some good banking business. (Use this year's date.)

On March 1st, Heidi deposited $19.29 that she had earned from babysitting jobs.

Heidi sold her old roller skates and some books and records in a sidewalk sale for $16.00. She deposited this money on June 16th.

From her allowance, Heidi saved $7.50, which she deposited on July 1st.

Grandmother Harrison mailed Heidi a check for $22.00 for back-to-school expenses. Heidi deposited it on August 2nd.

How much money did Heidi have in her checking account on September 1st? _____

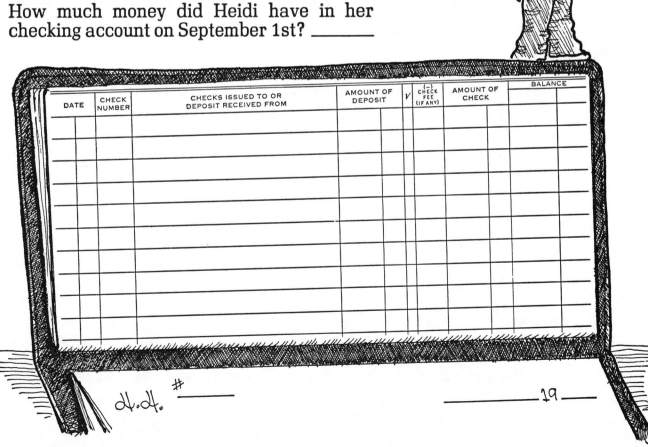

DATE	CHECK NUMBER	CHECKS ISSUED TO OR DEPOSIT RECEIVED FROM	AMOUNT OF DEPOSIT	√	(−) CHECK FEE (IF ANY)	AMOUNT OF CHECK	BALANCE

H. H. # _____   _____ 19 ___

Day By Day

PURPOSE: Conceiving and verbalizing by keeping a daily journal

PREPARATION

1. Ask each student to bring a notebook to be used *only* for keeping a daily journal.

2. Read several short excerpts from journals (such as the *Diary of Anne Frank*) to the class. Discuss the special kinds of thinking and writing that are peculiar to journal writing (i.e.: personal and private, but in this case, something that may be read by the teacher). Mention several kinds of things that students might want to record, such as daily happenings they'd like to remember, feelings, goals to work toward, new ideas, poems, etc.

PROCEDURE

1. Set aside a 5-10 minute period each day for students to write 3- or 4-sentence entries in their journals. Emphasize that the journals will not be corrected; however, the teacher may write a brief comment after a week's entries.

2. Ask students to date each entry. Encourage them to be neat, and to add any special drawings, cartoons, or hieroglyphics they wish. (They may also wish to address each entry, i.e.: "Dear Self," or "Dear [name].")

3. Collect journals once a week (or a few each day) to observe each student's progress in language skills and personal understanding. Special needs for skill development will become apparent in the process. (These journals also make an excellent basis for parent/teacher conferences.)

   Note: By all means, keep a daily journal yourself, and make it available for the students to read while you are reading theirs. Use it to set an example of interesting, humor-laced, meaningful writing. It's also a good way to let them know some of your feelings and to emphasize good values.

DEAR DIARY

PURPOSE: Writing a diary

PREPARATION

1. Reproduce copies of the "It's All in How You Write It" and the "Today Is The Day" work sheets.

PROCEDURE

1. Lead a class discussion of the value of keeping a diary, emphasizing such aspects as:

    1. personal pleasure,
    2. self-discipline,
    3. improvement in writing skills and style,
    4. having a permanent record of daily events,
    5. being able to read back over your own life story at a future time.

2. Read and discuss excerpts from the diaries of some famous people.

    Diary of an Edwardian Lady   *Diary of Anne Frank*
    Diary of Evelyn Waugh   *Diary of Tchaikovsky*

3. Distribute copies of the "It's All in How You Write It" work sheet.

4. Allow time for the work sheet to be read and answers to questions written.

5. Discuss ways people observe what is happening around them and develop sensitivity to people and events in their environments, and how this makes a difference in their attitudes and beliefs.

6. Distribute copies of "Today Is the Day" to be used as a homework assignment (and don't forget to plan time for follow-up).

IT'S ALL IN HOW YOU WRITE IT

Justin and Josephine are good friends. They live on the same street and are in the same grade. As they walked to school one day, they decided to share their diaries.

Here are some sample pages from each diary.

Monday, Oct. 10

We rode the bus to the zoo. It was a great field trip - I was fascinated by the baby elephant. Justin said that the snakes were hibernating and that is why they were so still - I'm not sure that is true.

Jennie and I ate lunch together and found we really have a lot in common. I made an A on my spelling test. Dad says he's really proud of my improvement.

Tues. Oct 11

Boy, was this day a downer! First, I forgot my lunch money. Next I did the wrong math pages for homework. Well, at least my teacher understood. After school I played kickball with Justin and Jackson - later the three of us went to the soda shop for ice cream cones. We seem to be getting along better now, I think it's because we're growing up.

Grandma came for supper and told us all about her new neighbors, the Seligman's, who moved from California.

Monday Oct 10

Went on a class field trip to the zoo. The animals were interesting.

Got my paper back from last week's spelling test.

We had guests for dinner and had a lot of special stuff to eat.

Tues. Oct. 11

Just a usual day - School was sort of boring. After school we played kick ball in the back yard and had fun.

After dinner I did homework, watched a little T.V., took my bath, and went to bed at my usual time.

Why is Josephine's diary more interesting to read than Justin's? _____

_____

_____

List three experiences that you know Justin had because Josephine recorded them in her diary.

1) _____

2) _____

3) _____

What advice would you give Justin? _____

_____

_____

_____

TODAY IS THE DAY

Write a page for your diary for today. Think over all the interesting things that happened, and decide what you want to remember.

Since a diary is a very personal bit of writing, you will want to use your space for only those things that you think are worth recording. Thoughts, questions, quotations, and feelings are important, too. Add a picture or two, if you like. Remember, it's **your** life you are writing about, and you are not a dull person!

Date _____ 19 ____

SPECIAL OCCASIONS

People who really care about other people learn to plan ahead to be able to bring happiness into the lives of others by remembering special occasions and events.

Make a list of the people you will want to remember in a special way during the next year. Note the date and the occasion, and the amount of money you think you will need for each person.

Example: Aunt Iris—Jan. 7th—Birthday—45¢ for a card

Name	Date	Occasion	Money

Add up the amounts you plan to spend for each occasion to find out how much money you should include in a budget for the year.

TELL THE WORLD

The date for the school Bake Sale and Pet Show has finally been set. You, of all people, have been appointed publicity chairman.

Here are the notes from the committee planning session. Read the notes carefully. Then, make a list of all the ways you can think of to get publicity.

Bake Sale and Pet Show Notes

- Sat., March 29, from 9 until 4 on the school playground - in the auditorium if it rains
- Admission free - everyone invited
- Something for all ages
- Pies, cakes, cookies, candy for sale
- Pet show on Tennis court at 1:00 PM

- Any student may enter pet in show
- Grand Prize is $25 gift certificate from Harding Pet Mall, and 2nd prize is 2 tickets to Sea Scape Marineland.

- Cokes, hot dogs, balloons, and stuffed toys will be for sale in booths

NOTES

... WITH A SIGN

Your very first job is to create a sign to be placed downtown on Main Street to advertise the big occasion.

Don't forget to check the committee notes for the correct time, place, and special events of the Bake Sale and Pet Show. Make the sign so attractive that everybody in town will want to come.

. . . IN THE NEWSPAPER

Use the committee notes from "Tell The World" to write an article to appear in the local newspaper. Then, create a five-sentence classified ad to appear in the same edition.

Remember to include all information related to the event in both the article and the ad.

A GRAND TIME WAS HAD BY ALL

Well, you did such a marvelous job as publicity chairman of the Bake Sale/Pet Show that you have been asked to write the first report to go on file in the official school Record Book.

In addition to the time, place, and other information included in the committee notes, here is the information you will need to include in the report.

- 725 people attended
- $940.00 was collected
- 46 pets were entered in the pet show
- first prize went to Billy Boner's poodle
- second prize went to Kristen Dalton's calico cat
- next year, the hot dog booth should be open earlier as many people said they would like to eat lunch before the pet show

_____

_____

_____

_____

_____

_____

_____

_____

_____

_____

_____

_____

_____

WRITING FOR EVERYDAY LIVING
COMPETENCY REVIEW

1. Number the parts of a letter from 1 to 5 to show the order in which they appear in a good business letter.

    ____ body
    ____ signature
    ____ heading
    ____ closing
    ____ greeting

2. Circle the name of the part of a letter that is most apt to be different in a friendly letter and a social note.

    signature
    body
    closing

3. Draw a line through the information that would not be presented by a graph or diagram.

    daily temperature
    stock market gains
    daily news events

4. Circle the phrase that tells what a poster or sign is usually designed to do.

    communicate a message
    entertain a group
    test ability

5. Circle the word that names the most commonly used source for securing geographical information.

    encyclopedia
    map
    dictionary

6. If you were lost in a large shopping center, which of the following would be most helpful to you?

    ____ listing of all the shops
    ____ map of the shopping center
    ____ local newspaper

7. Draw a line through the word that asks for information not usually requested on a personal identification form.

    weight
    hobbies
    height

8. Circle the information that would not be important on a job application form.

    experience
    education
    food preferences

9. Number these words to show the order in which they would usually appear on a job application form.

    __ address __ age
    __ name   __ experience

10. Underline the phrase that best completes the definition of a contract.

    A contract form usually tells what a person:
    agrees to do;
    dreams of doing someday;
    has done in the past.

11. Draw a line through the information not needed on an order blank.

> price of item ordered
> what you plan to do with the item
> your address

12. Underline the best definition of a memo.

> a friendly note
> a short message written to give specific information
> a form for organizing and reporting factual knowledge

13. Underline the phrase that best completes the definition of a biography.

> A biography is:
> the story of a person's life written by the person himself;
> the story of a long-ago time and place;
> the story of a person's life, written by someone else.

14. Draw a line through the information that would not be found in a bibliography.

> the name of a book publisher
> the address of an author
> the address of a publisher

15. Circle the sentence that tells what happens when money is deposited in a bank checking account.

> Money is taken from the checking account.
> Money is added to the checking account.
> Interest is paid on money in the checking account.

16. Underline the phrase that best completes this sentence.

> A good newspaper ad:
> creates interest in the product or service advertised;
> is beautiful to look at;
> should always be run at least three times.

17. Number these sentences to show the order in which they should appear in a report of a pet show.

> ____ The pet show was a huge success.
> ____ Next year's show should be in a larger room.
> ____ The pet show was held in the school cafeteria at 10:00 a.m. on Wednesday, January 16.

18. Draw a line through the information that would not be important in a report of a pet show.

> 46 pets were entered in the show.
> The grand parade was the highlight of the show.
> I had a headache and had to take an aspirin.

Answer Key
&
Glossary

WRITING

ANSWERS FOR COMPETENCY REVIEWS

I. Using Words and Phrases

1. grow, eat
2. under
3. punch, sneeze, nail, duck
4. tree-tall; bear-furry; day-cloudy
5. carefully, quietly, often, suddenly
6. body (n, a); clown (n, v, a); name (n, v, a)
7. flew; all; nothing
8. hit; bother
9. 2, 1, 3; 1, 3, 2
10. foxes; chiefs; children; men
11. the mice's tails; Shirley's bag; baby's rattle; the men's room
12. tall; generous; spicy
13. abbreviations: MST, F, Mr., Dr., U.S.A.F., Colo., Gen., G., S.
    contractions: o'clock, won't, wasn't, You're, I'm, don't, We're, They're, can't, didn't, I'll, don't
14. quick as a wink; killed two birds with one stone
15. H, B, E, C, I, A, J, G, F, D

II. Using Technical Writing Skills

1. "Horrors! Someone has stolen my hat, my gloves, and my wig," said Horace LeBlanc. "Hasn't anyone seen the thief?"
2. birthday; January; He; nine; mother; Sesame Street; he; Monopoly; Grandfather; Joey.
3. usually; nickel; popular; separate
4. Do you know my uncle?
5. Stop that nonsense now!
6. Are you a robot?
7. B; A; C; A; D; C; B
8. A toad needs a pocket to be put into.
9. 3; 6; 2; 1; 5; 4
10. H; G; C; D; A; F; B; E

III. Composition and Original Writing

1. biographies of people who live there
2. interviews with the mayor's friends and neighbors
3. 2, 1, 3
4. B
5. I can't hear you./Dumb.
6. Antique Swiss clock for sale—China face, crystal case, gold inlay, fine chimes
7. B, E, A, D, C
8. F, E, A, B, C, D
9. Little Boy Blue,/Where are you?
10. 5
11. Limerick—AABBA
    Couplets—AABB
    Free Verse—none
12. L—Dean's Strawberry Jam
    T—The Tale of Benjamin
    C—Wash out!
13. Yesterday, Greg and Tina were on their way to buy lettuce, celery, and carrots when they ran into Mrs. Wilson.

IV. Writing for Everyday Living

1. 3, 5, 1, 4, 2
2. body
3. daily news events
4. communicate a message
5. map
6. map of the shopping center
7. hobbies
8. food preferences
9. name, address, age, experience
10. agrees to do
11. what you plan to do with the item
12. a short message written to give specific information
13. the story of a person's life, written by someone else
14. the address of an author
15. Money is added to the checking account.
16. creates interest in the product or service advertised
17. 2, 3, 1
18. I had a headache and had to take an aspirin.

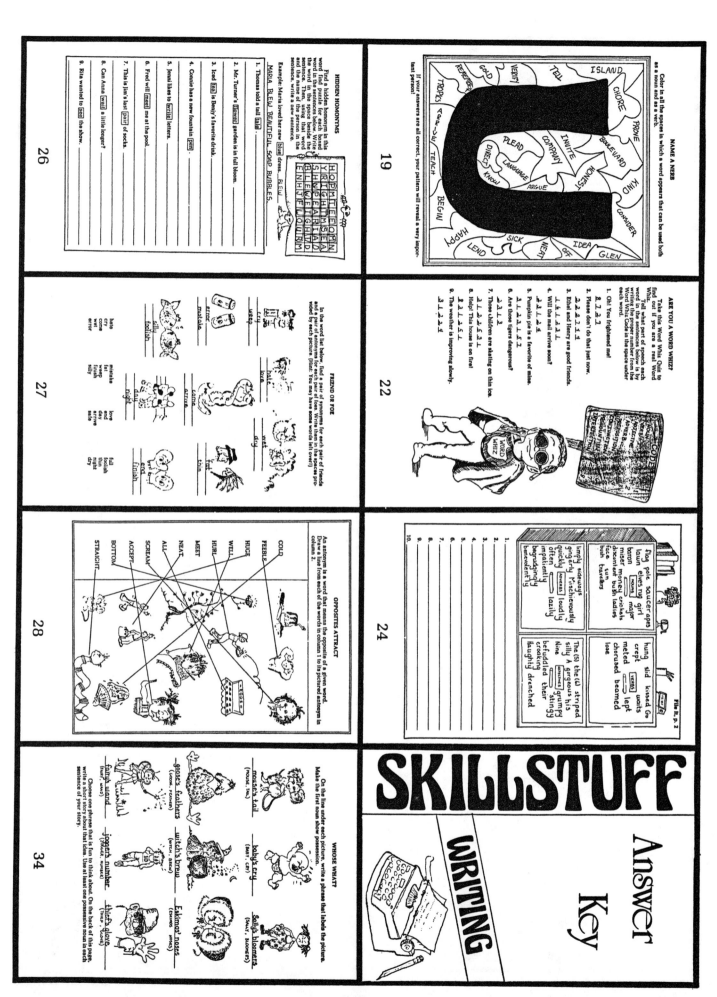

19

NAME A VERB

Color in all the spaces in which a word appears that can be used both as a noun and as a verb.

If your answers are all correct, your pattern will reveal a very important last person!

(Puzzle words: ISLAND, CHORE, TELL, VERIFY, GOLD, REMEMBER, PROVE, BOULEVARD, KIND, CONSIDER, INVITE, COMPANY, HONEST, PLEAD, LANGUAGE, DIRECT, ARGUE, KNOW, TEACH, ARRIVE, TROPICS, BEGIN, HAPPY, LEND, NEAT, OFF, SICK, IDEA, GLEN)

22

ARE YOU A WORD WHIZ?

Take this Word Whiz Quiz to find out if you are a real Word Whiz.

Tell what part of speech each word is in the sentences below by writing the proper number from the Word Whiz Code in the space under each word.

CODE: NOUN, PRONOUN, VERB, ADJECTIVE, ADVERB, PREPOSITION, CONJUNCTION, INTERJECTION

1. Oh! You frightened me!
2. Please don't do that just now.
3. Ethel and Henry are good friends.
4. Will the mail arrive soon?
5. Pumpkin pie is a favorite of mine.
6. Are those tigers dangerous?
7. Those children are skating on thin ice.
8. Help! This house is on fire!
9. The weather is improving slowly.

24

Fill in, p. 2

[word list: flag, pole, saucer, apes, lawn, elves, rug, girl, baron, major — NOUNS; crept, hung, sid, kissed, Ge, waits, miser, money, crickets, meted, chorused, lept, discontent, bush, ladies, beamed, lose, face, sun — VERBS; imply, sideways, gingerly, mischievously, quickly, loudly, often, impatiently, begrudgingly, benevolently, lazily — ADVERBS; The (5) the (4) striped, silly, A gorgeous, his, nine, grumpy, befuddled, their, stingy, croaking, haughty, drenched — ADJECTIVES]

1. ____
2. ____
3. ____
4. ____
5. ____
6. ____
7. ____
8. ____
9. ____
10. ____

26

HIDDEN HOMONYMS

Find a hidden homonym in this word find puzzle for each boxed word in the sentences below. Write the word beside the sentence. Then, using that word and the name of the person in the sentence, write a new sentence.

Example: Maria loved her new [blue] dress.
MARIA BLEW BEAUTIFUL SOAP BUBBLES.

1. Thomas told us a tall [tale]. ____
2. Mr. Turner's [flower] garden is in full bloom. ____
3. Iced [tea] is Benjy's favorite drink. ____
4. Connie has a new fountain [pen]. ____
5. Jenni likes to [write] letters. ____
6. Fred will [meet] me at the pool. ____
7. This is Jim's last [pair] of socks. ____
8. Can Anna [wait] a little longer? ____
9. Rita wanted to [see] the show. ____

```
H O P M T E E A M N
Y R I G H T M S E A
S H N P E A R I A D
B L E W F L O W R M
E N H J F L G U H M
```

27

FRIEND OR FOE

In the word list below, find a pair of synonyms for each pair of friends and a pair of antonyms for each pair of foes. Write them in the spaces provided by each picture. (Hint: You may have some words left over!)

cry / weep
silly / foolish
hate / love
come / arrive
day / night
wet / dry
finish
thin / fat

Word list:
hate	mistake
cry	weep
come	finish
wet	silly
error	
	love
	end
	day
	arrive
	safe
full	
foolish	
thin	
night	
dry	

28

OPPOSITES ATTRACT

An antonym is a word that means the opposite of a given word. Draw a line from each of the words in column 1 to its pictured antonym in column 2.

COLD
FEEBLE
HUGE
WELL
HURL
MEET
NEAT
ALL
SCREAM
ACCEPT
BOTTOM
STRAIGHT

SKILLSTUFF

Answer Key

WRITING

34

WHOSE WHAT?

On the line under each picture, write a phrase that labels the picture. Make the first noun show possession.

- mouse's tail (MOUSE, TAIL)
- goose's feathers (GOOSE, FEATHERS)
- witch's brew (WITCH, BREW)
- baby's cry (BABY, CRY)
- Eskimo's noses (ESKIMO, NOSES)
- fairy's wand (FAIRY, WAND)
- jogger's number (JOGGER, NUMBER)
- thief's glove (THIEF, GLOVE)
- Sally's bloomers (SALLY, BLOOMERS)

Choose one phrase that is fun to think about. On the back of this page, write a short story about that idea. Use at least one possessive noun in each sentence of your story.

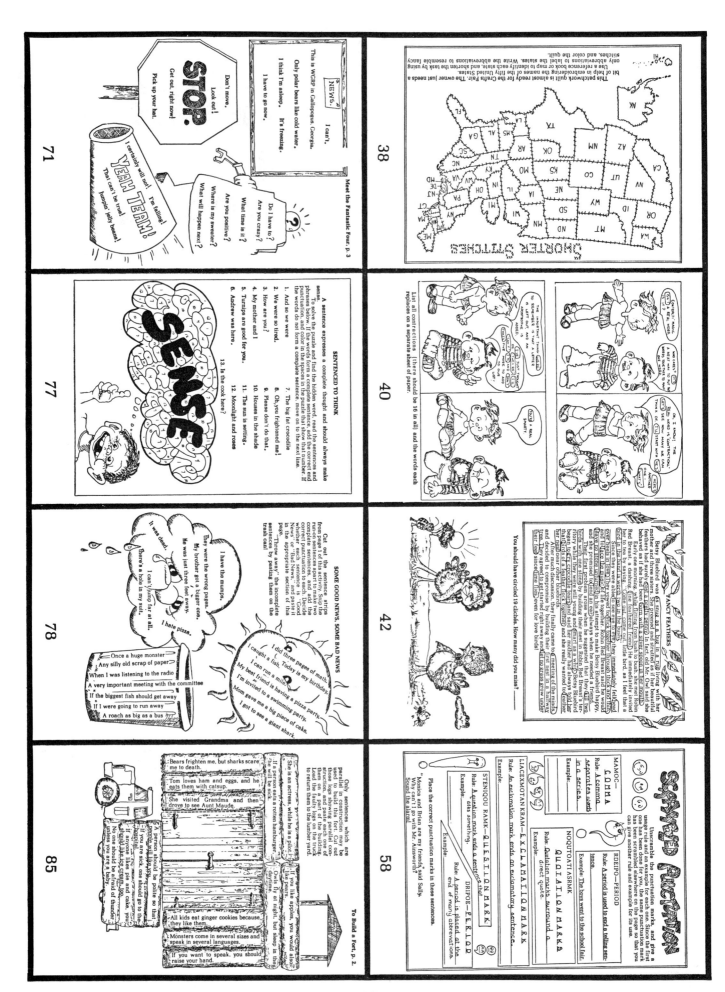

38 — SHORTER STITCHES

This patchwork quilt is almost ready for the Crafts Fair. The owner just needs a bit of help in embroidering the names of the fifty United States. Use a reference book or map to identify each state, and shorten the task by using only abbreviations to label the states. Write the abbreviations to resemble fancy stitches, and color the quilt.

---

71 — Meet the Fantastic Four, p. 3

NEWS

I can't.
I have to go now.
I think I'm asleep.
It's freezing.
Only polar bears like cold water.
This is WCRP in Gallipogus, Georgia.

Don't move.
Look out!
Pick up your hat.

STOP.
Get out, right now!

I certainly will not!
I'm failing!
That can't be true!
Jumpin' jelly beans!
YEAH TEAM!

What will happen next?
Where is my sweater?
What time is it?
Are you crazy?
Do I have to?

40

List all contractions (there should be 16 in all) and the words each replaces on a separate sheet of paper.

---

77 — SENTENCED TO THINK

A sentence expresses a complete thought and should always make sense. To solve the puzzle find the hidden word, read the sentences and phrases below. If the words form a complete sentence, add the correct end punctuation, and color in the space that has that number. If the words do not form a complete sentence, move on to the next line.

1. And so we were.
2. We were so tired.
3. How are you?
4. My mother and I
5. Turnips are good for you.
6. Andrew was here.
7. The big fat crocodile
8. Oh, you frightened me!
9. Please don't do that.
10. Houses in the shade
11. The sun is setting.
12. Moonlight and roses
13. Is the cook here?

SENSE

---

42 — FANCY FEATHERS

Betsy Bluebird was as snug as a bug living with her mother and three sisters. ... You should have circled 19 clichés. How many did you miss?

---

58 — SCRAMBLED PUNCTUATION

Unscramble the punctuation marks, and give a usage rule and an example for each one. Since the first one has been done for you, you can give another rule and an example for its use.

MAMOC — COMMA
Rule: A comma separates words in a series.
Example:

NOQUOTAIIASRMK — QUOTATION MARKS
Rule: Quotation marks surround a direct quote.
Example:

RDEIPO—PERIOD
Rule: A period is used to end a telling sentence.
Example: The boss went to the school fair.

STENIQOU RAMK—QUESTION MARK
Rule: A question mark asks something.
Example:

DRIPOE-PERIOD
Rule: A period is placed at the end of many abbreviations.
Example:

LIACEXMOTAN KRAM—EXCLAMATION MARK
Rule: An exclamation mark ends an exclamatory sentence.
Example:

Place the correct punctuation marks in these sentences.
"Monica and Brian are my friends," said Sally.
Why can't I go with Mr. Ainsworth?
Sound the alarm!

---

78 — SOME GOOD NEWS, SOME BAD NEWS

Cut out the sentence strips from page 1 of this activity. Snip the run-on sentences apart to make two complete sentences, and add the correct punctuation to each. Decide whether each sentence is "Good News" or "Bad News," and paste it in the appropriate section of this page. "Throw away" the incomplete sentences by pasting them on the trash can!

I have the mumps.
They were the wrong pages.
My brother got a bigger one.
He was just three feet away.
It was dead.
I can/jump far at all.
there's a hole in my suit.
I hate pizza.

Once a huge monster
Any silly old scrap of paper
When I was listening to the radio
A very important meeting with the committee
If the biggest fish should get away
If I were going to run away
A roach as big as a bus

I did three pages of math.
I can run a mile.
Today is my birthday.
My best friend is having a pizza party.
I'm invited to a swimming party.
Mom gave me a big piece of cake.
got to see a giant shark.

---

85 — To Build a Fort, p. 2

Only sentences which are parallel in construction may be used to build this fort. Cut out those logs showing parallel construction, and paste each one of them on a part of the building. Load the faulty logs on the truck to return them to the lumber yard.

Bears frighten me, but sharks scare me to death.
Tom loves ham and eggs, and he eats them with catsup.
She visited Grandma and then drove to see Aunt Maude.
She is an actress, while he is a pilot.
A person should be polite so that people will like you.
If you are sick, one should go to the hospital.
No one should be afraid of thunder unless you are a baby.
Ducks fly at night, but sleep in the daytime.
If you like apples, you would also like pears.
All kids eat ginger cookies because they like them.
Monsters come in several sizes and speak in several languages.
If you want to speak, you should raise your hand.

87 — IDEAS IN ORDER

Number the sentences below to show the natural time order in which they occurred. Then, rewrite them in paragraph form in the space below. (Don't forget to indent the first line!)

2. Next, we tried to decide if we should go by air or by train.
5. Later, we agreed that all our time and effort had been well spent because this plan pleased both of us.
1. First, we spent hours making careful plans for our trip.
4. Then, we discovered this wonderful fly-and-drive package that allowed us to do both.
3. Meanwhile, we began collecting road maps and travel brochures.
6. Finally, the plans were complete, the bags were packed, and we were ready to go.

Write a paragraph telling about a trip you would like to take with your family.

124 — EGG-OMANIA

Egg-omania is "cracking" people up! They are putting one "over easy" on their friends! See how many of the eggs you can "unscramble."

egg + ... = Exit
"egg" + "sit" = "egg-sit" = EXIT!

1. ... = exit
2. ... = exam
3. ... = expand
4. ... = expire
5. ... = explain
... = extent

The sentences at the top of this page are true puns. Look up the meaning of the word pun in the dictionary. Then use the space here to write a pun or two of your own!

108 — PART TO PART, FROM THE START

This is a story, but its parts are not in order. Read each part carefully. Then, beginning with the part that starts the story, draw a squiggle line to connect each part to the part that follows it until the whole story is connected. BEWARE!! One part does not belong. Cross it out, and do not connect it at all!

[Write your title here.]

Kim had to give Chip a bath.
Chip ran to the bath with a bone.
She got some soap and a big tub of water.
She made a tub of bubbles.
Bats like bubble baths.
He did not like baths.
Chip saw the bath and hid.
Chip ended up clean and happy.

130

On this design page, color each space that shows a number you have circled. If you have circled all the right numbers, you'll discover a new friend!

Hyperbole Hysteria, p. 2

115 — As Smart As A Whip!

Are you? Prove it. See if your can complete these similes.

As fresh as a daisy
As blind as a bat
As good as gold
As sly as a fox
As cool as a cucumber
As sweet as daisy
As dead as a doornail
As clear as mud
As stubborn as a mule
As quick as a wink
As pale as a ghost
As clean as a whistle
As funny as a barrel of monkeys
As pretty as a picture

How did a whip get to be smart? In these spaces, copy four of your favorite similes from the list above. Beside each, write your guess as to how this simile came to be a common figure of speech.

In the two spaces below, make up some similes of your own.

CRACK!

142 — RHYME IN TIME

The rhythm of poetry makes it especially fun to say and hear. Often, the last words of the lines form a rhyming pattern. Read these poems, and use matching colors to underline the lines that rhyme. Then, mark the lines that are the same color with the same letter.

I beg you, please,
Try not to sneeze.
It makes a breeze,
And spreads disease!

The day I tried
To eat a whole cake
Of a stomach ache!

"The day I tried
To eat a whole cake
I nearly died
Of a stomach ache!"

Jack be nimble
Jack be quick
Jack jump over
The candlestick!

On a morning hung heavy with fog
Quite early, I went for a jog.
I trudged along,
Still mostly asleep.
I neglected to leap,
And landed my head on a log!

Candy
Is dandy!
Stew...
Phew!!

Little Bo Peep
Has lost her sheep
And can't tell where to find them.
Leave them alone and they'll come home
Wagging their tails behind them.

117 — UFO'S (UNIDENTIFIED FIGURES OF SPEECH)

Concentrate your laser-powered focus beam on these UFO'S so you can identify them with one of these friendly alien groups!

Mark each UFO with its identifying initial shield. (A few UFO'S may be members of more than one group!)

S Simile
O Onomatopoeia
M Metaphor
P Personification
A Alliteration

153 — The Incredible Proof Prince

Once there was a Valiant prince who traveled the Kingdom of the Written Word making wrong things WRite. He was called the Incredible Proof Prince because he made it his business to ferret out trouble here and there, always leaving one of his special magic prints on an exact trouble spot, causing it to turn out just WRite.

He was loved by everyone in the kingdom—everyone except the Duke of Error. The Duke was a rotten fellow who did what he could to cast evil spellings and cause misunderstanding, so that travelers would become hopelessly lost and confused.

Finally, the incredible proof prince could stand it no longer. He became enraged and abused you cause confusion in this kingdom with your Error! Nevermore shall you cause confusion in this kingdom! With that he drew his powerful proofreader's pen-sword and reduced the Duke of Error to an ordinary lower-case dash, no longer heralded by staunch exclamation points, but left hanging by fretting threats to the comma of a cowardly question mark.

Long live the Incredible Proof Prince!!

Allegory—a story presented on a superficial level which parallels and illustrates a deeper meaning.

Alliteration—the repetition of one initial sound in several words within a phrase.

Annotation—a short, critical commentary of a book.

Ballad—a narrative poem which uses simple language and a refrain; is usually intended to be sung, and is often a folk tale.

Bibliography—a formal listing of books, usually on a specific subject, giving author, title, city, publisher, and date.

Characterization—the description of a person through the use of any of a variety of literary techniques.

Cinquain—a five-line poetic form which follows this pattern: line 1, a one-word subject or idea; line 2, two descriptive adjectives; line 3, three related action verbs; line 4, three or four words that give a personal reaction; line 5, a one-word synonym for the first line.

Cliché—a trite, overused expression.

Climax—the point at which a story, poem, or drama reaches its most intense emotional point; culmination.

Colloquialism—an informal, conversational word or phrase which may be idiomatic or include slang and/or jargon native to a certain group of people.

Couplet—a two-line poetic form in which both lines use the same rhyme scheme and meter.

Dialogue—the conversation between two or more characters.

Diamante—a seven-line poetry form which follows this pattern: lines 1 and 7, a noun or pronoun; lines 2 and 6, two adjectives; lines 3 and 5, three participles; line 4, four nouns.

Edit—to make a written work ready for public consumption by correcting and polishing it.

Editorial—a newspaper article which usually expresses the editor's view (or another person's view) of a current situation.

Epic—an extensive narrative poem which celebrates an event or praises the adventures of a hero important to the history of a culture group.

Epigraph—a quotation or motto found at the beginning of a chapter or a book which is related to the material that follows it.

Epilogue—a short speech made directly to the audience at the end of a play, or a concluding section at the end of a literary work which usually deals with the future of the characters from that work.

Epitaph—a short literary piece epitomizing and praising a deceased person.

Essay—a short, personal literary

compositon which usually gives the views of the writer.

Expository—a kind of writing in which meaning or intent is clearly stated.

Fable—a story about legendary people and events.

Figure of Speech—a phrase in which words are used to create a forceful or dramatic feeling.

First Draft—the first written format of a literary work.

Flashback—an explanatory episode which interrupts a play or story to show something that happened in the past.

Footnote—a note found at the bottom of a page which cites a reference for a designated part of the text.

Free Verse—poetry which follows no conventional rhythm pattern or rhyme scheme.

Glossary—a listing in the back of a book in which words are defined in terms of their usage within that book.

Haiku—a Japanese poetry form which consists of three lines; the first and third having 5 syllables, and the second having 7 syllables.

Idiom—a phrase that conveys a meaning different from the exact definitions of the words used in it.

Imagery—the employment of figures of speech or vivid descriptions; the collection of such representations in a literary work.

Index—an alphabetical listing of terms in a book, accompanied by the page numbers on which each is found.

Irony—an expression which makes a deliberate contrast between what appears to be so and what actually is.

Jargon—the specialized language of a group, profession, or fellowship of some sort.

Journal—a daily record; diary.

Legend—an unverified, popular narrative story handed down from the past.

Limerick—a five-line, light nonsense or humorous verse which usually uses the rhyme scheme a-a-b-b-a.

Lyric—poetry which is melodic in form, and personal and sensual in nature.

Metaphor—a figure of speech that implies comparison between two things which are basically unlike.

Monologue—a speech in which there is only one speaker.

Mood—the feeling that a composition produces in its reader.

Myth—a story which orignated in a preliterate society, usually dealing with supernatural beings or heroes.

Narrative—a story or description of events.

Ode—a long, lyric, rhymed poem that often addresses and praises in exalted terms some person, object, or quality.

Onomatopoeia—the formation of a word that sounds like what it describes.

Outline—a formal summarization of information that follows a definite grammatical format.

Parable—a simple story which illustrates a moral or religious truth.

Parody—a work that intentionally and broadly mimics, and thereby ridicules, the characteristic work of another.

Personification—the act of endowing an inanimate object or abstraction with human qualities.

Plot—a series of events which make up the outline or action of a literary work.

Point of View—the position from which something is told; the narrator's position.

Précis—a concise summary of the essential facts; writing which is very concise and to the point.

Prologue—the poetry or prose that introduces a play or a narrative, usually set off from the main body of the work.

Proofread—to carefully check over a written work for errors.

Pun—a literary form which is a play on words, either on a word which has several meanings, or on words that sound alike.

Quatrain—a four-line stanza or poem which usually has a rhyming pattern.

Report—a detailed account of information or an event presented in a formal, organized format.

Review—a critical work (usually in written form) which reports on a book, a play, or some form of entertainment.

Rhyme Scheme—any of various rhyming formats or patterns used in poetry.

Satire—a literary work of any form which employs wit, derision, or irony to point up folly, stupidity, or sin.

Script—the written text of a play, show, or movie.

Simile—a figure of speech in which two unlike things are compared; introduced by *like* or *as*.

Sonnet—a poem composed of an octave (8 lines) and a sestet (6 lines) in which the complete statement and resolution of a theme are related.

Spoonerism—an unintentional transposition of sounds in spoken language.

Summary—a condensed, concise restatement of information.

Tanka—a Japanese verse form of five lines, of which the first and third lines have 5 syllables, and the rest have 7 syllables.

Vignette—a delicate, subtle, literary sketch; a decorative design sometimes found at the beginning or end of a chapter or a book.

Vocabulary—all the words used and understood by a person or a group.

WRITING

TABLE OF CONTENTS

- Look for new words in every book you read. Practice pronouncing and writing them.

- Learn to spell one new word every day.

- Read catalog descriptions to find words used to influence consumers to buy catalog items. Use the words in some written form within three days.

- Pick a word.
  —Write rhyming words.
  —Use it to make new words.
  —List synonyms.
  —List antonyms.
  —List homonyms.
  —List heteronyms.
  —Write a paragraph about the word.
  —Look up the meaning in your dictionary.
  —Write it like it feels.
  —Use it as the basis for a collage.
  —Challenge a friend to spell it.

- Write a play you'd like for your class to present. Be sure to make the dialogue interesting, entertaining, and original.

- Play Scrabble, Word Bingo, Spell-O, and Boggle.

- Make regular deposits in your own word and phrase bank. Use these as starters, and add more of your own.

Linking Words:	however	moreover	therefore	furthermore
	hence	meanwhile	whereas	nevertheless

  Words That Show Time Order:

later	before	finally	earlier
first	then	next	afterward

- Make lists of words and phrases that:
  —Add pizzazz
  —Create excitement
  —Describe
  —Arouse curiosity
  —Demand attention
  —Build suspense

- Write to a pen pal, preferably one your own age who lives in another country. Use interesting and descriptive words and phrases to tell about yourself, your home, and your own particular interests.

2

- Use a guide to free and inexpensive learning materials to find three sets of information materials you would like to have. Select materials on topics you know little or nothing about, and write letters requesting the materials. If you don't have a current, updated guide, you need one. A good one is:

   Free and Inexpensive Learning Materials by George Peabody College for Teachers. (Available from Incentive Publications, Inc., P.O. Box 120189, Nashville, TN 37212, at a cost of $4.50 plus $1.00 for shipping and handling charges.)

- Keep a diary—make it personal and private.

- Become a list-maker. Start with lists of:
  —Things to do
  —Wishes
  —TV and radio programs
  —Names and addresses
  —Important events
  —Places to go
  —Things to see
  —Budgets

- Design your own greeting cards complete with unique and original messages from you!

- Pick out and pronounce the rhyming words as you read poetry.

- Read cook books, game books, and other books giving directions in a sequential manner. Make a list of the words used frequently to tell the reader "what to do," "when to do," and "how to do."

- Make a list of twenty careers that interest you. Use your dictionary or thesaurus to find one or more unusual synonyms for each of the careers.

- Write a letter to your senator or representative about a matter of concern to you. Use ten words that you've never used in a letter before.

- Look in the Yellow Pages of the telephone book to find words frequently used in ads. Just for fun, make a list of all the three-syllable words that are used more than three times on one page.

- Daydream, and write down your dreams.

- Make a list of your friends and family members and their birthday. Send one of your original greeting cards to each one on the appropriate day.

- Hang a large piece of paper on a wall in your room. Each time you learn a new word, write it in fancy script on the paper. Use lots of different colors to make your "Word Wall" interesting and attractive.

stationery, tablets, pads, notebooks
acetate
file folders
fabric
index cards
tissues
grocery sacks, shopping bags
gift bags
paper towels
kites
your hands and feet (or someone else's, with
    their permission)
bodies
gift-wrap paper
canvas
cardboard, posterboard, tagboard
construction paper
tissue paper
cakes
cookies
adding machine tape
old window shade
plastic tablecloth
hats
T-shirts
old lamp shades
paper plates and cups
wooden spoons
shirt boards
*bath tubs
*sinks
 leaves, stones, and rocks
*shovels
*mirrors
*windows
 toilet paper
 wood strips, shingles
*cookie sheets
*pot lids
*sidewalks, streets
 bricks and concrete blocks
*drinking glasses
*sunglasses
*dust pans (make good wings)
*plastic plates, cups, and glasses
*formica table tops
*glass table tops
*refrigerator doors
 old wallpaper
 fingers of a glove
 boxes
* Be sure to use water-soluble writing
  materials on these!

pencil
pen
chalk
paint
soap
shoe polish
shaving cream
toothpaste
feather
lipstick
cake frosting
yarn or twine
glue
mud
twigs and sticks
paint brushes
sponges
ribbon
string
tape
finger and toes
shells
stones
syrup
pudding
salt
buttons
rope
beans
seeds
cereal
nails and tacks
rags and cotton balls
large-headed pins
blocks
letters cut from magazines, newspaper,
    bulletins, and brochures
paper punched holes
needle and thread
embroidery thread
dental floss
words cut from greeting cards
paper clips (glued together or laid end to end)
string beans
spaghetti
pretzel sticks
whipped cream
crayons
wet ashes
felt markers
press-on letters

4

The famous ballerina leaped into the air . . .
A huge black bear lumbered toward the highway . . .
Out of the darkness and into the campfire's light came . . .
Please don't say . . .
In magnificent splendor . . .
Suddenly, the sky lit up . . .
A piercing scream broke the stillness . . .
Silly, I know, but . . .
The excitement of the midway became contagious . . .
I don't believe in magic pencils, but . . .
The crocodile opened his jaws wide . . .
Senators should be careful about what they eat . . .
The train roared on into the night . . .
In a split second . . .
The unbelievably beautiful sunset . . .
The fog set in at midday . . .
Snips and snails and sand pails . . .
Miles and miles of forbidding coast line stretched ahead . . .
A house just as desolate as the one before . . .
Where the tornado hit . . .
I'm sorry, but that's just how it is . . .
A ghost walked here last night . . .
The boat slowly pulled away from the shore . . .
Man's best friend is . . .
Women's best friend is . . .
The drill captain roared . . .
As flood waters continued to rise . . .
Right in my own backyard, I . . .
The driver looked away for just a second . . .
A strange smell came from the swamp . . .
The whole horizon was covered by a dark cloud . . .
The stone simply would not budge . . .
I became more frightened with every step . . .
Under the giant mushroom . . .
The day the teacher overslept, we . . .
We played this crazy game in which you had to . . .
It all started when . . .
All the kids on the block waited anxiously . . .
The strangest looking dog I've ever seen . . .
The curtains in back of the dusty window parted slowly, and . . .
If I live to be one hundred and four, I'll never . . .
The last bar on the cage gave way, and the lion . . .
The flashlight was shining directly into my tent . . .
The ground began to sink down, down, down . . .
He's been missing for more than two days . . .
Suddenly, the lantern sputtered and went out . . .
A pocket knife is the only clue to . . .
More than anything in the world, she wanted to . . .
Gold!!! . . .
Under the pillow was a note saying . . .
Gigantic footprints led right up to the . . .
As the band began to play, . . .
Caught in the act again! . . .
Get me out of here, please . . .
The label said, "Open at your own risk." . . .
I felt my body shrinking, shrinking . . .
He stuck his hand in the opening, and pulled out . . .
The whole town was in an uproar . . .

When the little fish asked the leviathan, "Are you ill?" he replied, "No, I'm whale."
Did you hear about the smart pole vaulter who really had the jump on things?
A silly lady is a dumb belle.
A swimming animal that barks is a dog fish.
"Dash it all!" exclaimed the runner.
The ruling animal is the reign-deer.
An octopus is a cat with eight sides.
Said the scissors-happy film director, "Cut! Cut!"
When asked why he was being spanked, the confused child said, "Beats me!"
A lost puppy is a dog gone.
"Don't drop the eggs," cracked the grocer.
Did you hear about the snobbish robbery victim who was really stuck up?
"I love all people," said the cannibal.
If your refrigerator is running, you should try to catch it!
A well is a deep subject.
As the lawyer said, "Just in case."
Said the golfer as he searched for his lost ball, "I don't know where I putt it."
A kindergarten teacher tries to make little things count.
Said the grizzly, "I can't bear it any more."
"I always let things slide," said the trombonist.
The dentist said, "My occupation is very filling."
"Could you please hurry?" said the man on his way to the cleaners. "I have a pressing engagement."
My cookbook certainly is exciting—it contains such stirring events.
A teacher without students has no class.
The baker really got a rise out of that.
The largest ants in the world are gi-ants.
That butcher is really a cut above.
"See you around," said the circle.
When the salesman left, he said, "Buy, buy!"
The strangest creature I've ever seen is a spelling bee.
The author said, "Write on!"
A sign hanging on an old boat: "For sail."
The tailor said, "Will this outfit suit you, sir?"
A clockmaker always works overtime.
Another name for an angrily rising ocean is an emergent sea (emergency).
"I want no part of that," said the bald man.
A barber runs a clip joint.
"Hand it over," said the manicurist.
The shoemaker said, "That boot really has sole!"
The principal part of a lion is its mane.
The night watchman said, "I've never done a day's work."
Dawn breaks but never falls.
The astronomer said, "My business is looking up."
I thought that Dracula movie was a pain in the neck.
The farmer said, "Sow what?"
He could be a wonderful pianist except for two things—his hands.
A demon's favorite dessert is devil's food cake.
The seamstress said, "You're sew right!"
This horn isn't broken—it just doesn't give a hoot!
When the nuclear scientist went on vacation, he left a sign on his door that read, "Gone fission."
The surgeon said, "I'll keep you in stitches."
Did you hear about the clergyman who wanted to make a parson-to-parson call?
If you stuck your head in a washing machine, you'd get brainwashed.
Niagara Falls but never breaks.
Did you hear about the wolf that got trapped in the laundry and became a wash and werewolf?

YOUNG WRITER'S CHECK LIST

Things to Write About	Date	Comments
Adventure		
Art		
Bodies of Water		
Books		
Communication		
Current Events		
Daydreams		
Families		
Fantasies		
Feelings		
Folklore		
the Future		
Gardening and Farming		
Geography		
Ghosts, Goblins, Witches, Fairies, Elves, and Trolls		
History		
Hobbies		
Holidays		
Land Formations		
Long Ago		
Manners		
Money		
Music		
Politics		
Problems		
Propaganda		
Religion		
Scenery		
Science		
Seasons		
Social Events		
Someone Else's Life		
Sports		
a Town, City, or Country		
Tragedy		
Transportation		
Travel		
Trivia		
the Unknown		
the Weather		
Your Life		

YOUNG WRITER'S CHECK LIST

Things to Write	Date	Comments
Ads		
Anecdotes		
Autobiographies		
Biographies		
Brochures		
Bulletins		
Cartoons		
Editorials		
Fables		
Feature Articles		
Graffiti		
Greeting Cards		
"How To" Booklets		
Jokes		
Letters		
Lists		
Minutes		
Myths		
Notes		
Novels		
Pamphlets		
Plays		
Poetry Forms		
Cinquains		
Couplets		
Free Verse		
Haiku		
Limericks		
Nursery Rhymes		
Odes		
Quatrains		
Sonnets		
Triplets		
Recipes		
Reports		
Riddles		
Science Fiction		
Slogans		
Songs		
Speeches		
Stories		
Tall Tales		

Feeling words	Holiday words	Election words
Sound words	Hate words	Size words
Color words	Adventure words	Shape words
Time words	Store words	War words
Friendly words	Family words	Peace words
Unfriendly words	Religious words	Nonsense words
Number words	Taste words	Season words
City words	Love words	Weather words
Country words	Hot words	Radio words
Day words	Cold words	Newspaper words
Night words	Circus words	TV words
Home words	Goodbye words	Career words
School words	Hello words	Baby words
Art words	Airplane words	Children words
Theater words	Train words	Teen-age words
Food words	Truck words	Adult words
Ocean words	Automobile words	Teacher words
Valley words	Swimming words	Pizzazz words
Hill words	Football words	Nature words
Jungle words	Golf words	Music words
Mountain words	Space words	Feminine words
Desert words	Advertising words	Masculine words
Seashore words	Tennis words	Library words
Shopping words	Baseball words	Tax words
Appreciation words	Basketball words	Mineral words
Disappointment words	Scratchy words	Plant words
Sad words	Yes words	Animal words
Glad words	No words	Hotel words
Clothing words		Restaurant words
Fashion words		Health words
Suspense words		Gym words
Fat words		Excitement words
Thin words		Fear words

Start your own "Big Book of Word Lists,"
and see how long it takes you to add 100 or
more categories with at least five words in
each category!

ability (power), **capacity** (condition)

accede (agree), **exceed** (surpass)

accept (receive), **except** (exclude)

adapt (adjust), **adopt** (accept)

advise (to give advice), **advice** (counsel or recommendation)

affect (to influence), **effect** (result)

all ready (completely prepared), **already** (previously)

allude (to refer to), **elude** (escape)

allusion (reference), **illusion** (false perception), **delusion** (false belief)

assure (to set a person's mind at ease), **insure** (guarantee life or property against harm), **ensure** (to secure from harm)

avenge (to achieve justice), **revenge** (retaliation)

averse (opposition on the subject's part), **adverse** (opposition against the subject's will)

avoid (shun), **prevent** (thwart), **avert** (turn away)

between (use when referring to two persons, places or things), **among** (use when referring to more than two places, persons, or things)

capital (seat of government), **capitol** (building)

censor (one who prohibits offensive material), **censure** (to criticize)

cite (to bring forward as support or truth), **quote** (to repeat exactly)

clench (to grip something tightly, as hand or teeth), **clinch** (to secure a bargain or something abstract)

complement (something that completes), **compliment** (an expression of praise)

compromise (a settlement in which each side makes concession), **surrender** (to yield completely)

confidant (one to whom secrets are told), **confidante** (a female confidant), **confident** (assured of success)

constant (unchanging), **continual** (repeated regularly), **continuous** (action without interruption)

contagious (transmissable by contact), **infectious** (capable of causing infection)

consul (a country's representative in a foreign country), **council** (a deliberative assembly), **councilor** (member of a deliberative body), **counsel** (to give advice), **counselor** (one who gives advice)

credible (plausible), **creditable** (deserving commendation), **credulous** (gullible)

deny (contradict), **refute** (to give evidence to disprove something), **repudiate** (to reject the validity of)

doubtless (presumption of certainty), **undoubtedly** (definite certainty)

elegy (a mournful poem), **eulogy** (a speech honoring a deceased person)

element (a basic assumption), **factor** (something that contributes to a result)

elicit (to evoke), **illicit** (unlawful)

emigrate (a single move by persons, used with *from*), **immigrate** (a single move by persons, used with *to*), **migrate** (seasonal movement)

eminent (prominent), **imminent** (soon to occur)

farther (literal distance), **further** (figurative distance)

fatal (causing death), **fateful** (affecting one's destiny)

feasible (clearly possible), **possible** (capable of happening)

fewer (refers to units capable of being individually counted), **less** (refers to collective quantities or to abstracts)

graceful (refers to movement), **gracious** (courteous)

impassable (impossible to traverse), **impassive** (devoid of emotion)

imply (to hint or suggest), **infer** (to draw conclusions based on facts)

incredible (unbelievable), **incredulous** (skeptical)

insignificant (trivial), **tiny** (small)

insinuate (to hint covertly), **intimate** (to imply subtly)

invoke (to call upon a higher power for assistance), **evoke** (to reawaken or inspire)

judical (pertaining to law), **judicious** (exhibiting sound judgment)

latter (the second of two things mentioned), **later** (subsequently)

lay (to put or place), **lie** (to recline)

10

likely (use when mere probability is involved), **apt** (use when a known tendency is involved)

mania (craze), **phobia** (fear)

may (use when strong sense of permission or possibility is involved), **might** (use when weak sense of permission or possibility is involved)

mutual (refers to intangibles of a personal nature between two parties), **reciprocal** (refers to a balanced relationship in which one action is made on account of or in return for another)

nauseated (to feel queasy), **nauseous** (causing queasiness)

oblige (to feel a debt of gratitude), **obligate** (under direct compulsion to follow a certain course)

official (authorized by a proper authority), **officious** (extremely eager to offer help or advice)

older (refers to persons and things), **elder** (refers only to persons)

on (used to indicate motion to a position), **onto** (very strongly conveys motion toward) **on to** (use when *on* is an adverb and *to* is a preposition)

oral (refers to the sense of "word of mouth;" cannot refer to written words), **verbal** (can refer to both written and spoken words)

partly (use when stress is placed on a part in contrast to the whole), **partially** (use when the whole is stressed, often indirectly)

people (refers to a large group of individuals considered collectively), **persons** (refers to a small, specific number), **public** (a group of people sharing a common interest)

persecute (to oppress or harass), **prosecute** (to initiate legal or criminal action against)

piteous (pathetic), **pitiable** (lamentable), **pitiful** (very inferior or insignificant)

practically (almost), **virtually** (to all intents)

precipitant (rash, impulsive), **precipitate** (to hurl downward), **precipitous** (extremely steep)

principal (chief), **principle** (basic law or truth)

quite (very), **quiet** (hushed)

rack (a framework; to be in great pain), **wrack** (destruction by violent means)

raise (to move upward; to build; to breed), **rear** (to bring up a child), **rise** (to ascend)

rare (refers to unusual value and quality of which there is a permanent small supply), **scarce** (refers to temporary infrequency)

ravage (to devastate or despoil), **ravish** (to take away by force; to rape)

recourse (an application to something for aid or support), **resource** (an available supply)

regretful (sorrowful), **regrettable** (something that elicits mental distress)

reluctant (unwilling), **reticent** (refers to a temperament or style that is characteristically silent or restrained)

repel (drive off; cause distaste or aversion), **repulse** (drive off; reject by means of discourtesy)

respectfully (showing honor and esteem), **respectively** (one at a time in order)

restive (resistance to control), **restless** (lacking repose)

seasonal (refers to what applies to or depends on a season), **seasonable** (refers to timeliness or appropriateness to a season)

sensual (used when referring to the gratification of physical [sexual] senses), **sensuous** (usually refers to senses involved in aesthetic gratification)

sit (to rest the body on the buttocks with the torso upright; usually intransitive), **set** (to put or place something; usually transitive)

specific (explicitly set forth), **particular** (not general or universal)

stationary (immovable), **stationery** (matched writing paper and envelopes

tasteful (exhibiting that which is proper or seemly in a social setting), **tasty** (having a pleasing flavor)

transient (refers to what literally stays for only a short time), **transitory** (sort-lived, impermanent)

turbid (muddy, dense; in turmoil), **turgid** (swollen; grandiloquent)

11

The following spelling rules are generalizations, and do not work all of the time. However, they are often true, and are valuable spelling aids.

1. Each syllable of a word must contain one sounded vowel. (al li ga tor)

2. A vowel is more likely to be pronounced short than long.

3. A vowel at the end of a one-syllable word is usually long. (be)

4. The final *e* in a one-syllable word is usually silent. (lake)

5. When *i* precedes *gh*, it is usually long. (bright)

6. *I* comes before *e* except after *c*, or when sounded like *a* as in *neighbor*, and *weigh*. (chief, receive)

7. Usually, a doubled consonant or vowel has one sound. (letter, boot)

8. When two vowels are together, the first one usually says its own name. (team)

9. The *ch* shound is often spelled *tch*. (catch)

10. The *j* sound is often spelled *dg* or *dge*. (dredging, smudge)

11. The *k* sound may be made by *c* or *ck*. (came, stack)

12. The *gh* combination is usually silent (dough, fright,) but sometimes it sounds like *f* (trough, laugh).

13. The consonants *c* and *h* are soft before *i, e,* and *y*; otherwise, they are hard. (go, gentle; center, car)

14. The ending *-ance* may also be spelled *-ence*. (endurance, presence)

15. The ending *-ous* may be used with an *e* or an *i*. (ominous, extraneous, delicious)

16. The ending *-tion* may be spelled *-cian, -sian, -sion,* or *-tian*. (station, physician, Prussian, decision, Dalmatian)

17. Pluralize a word that ends in *y* with a consonant before it by changing the *y* to *i* and adding *es*. (cry, cries)

18. The common prefixes *en-, in-,* and *un-* are not used interchangeably.

Amazing—incredible, unbelievable, improbable, fabulous, wonderful, fantastic, astonishing, astounding, extraordinary

Anger—enrage, infuriate, arouse, nettle, exasperate, inflame, madden

Angry—mad, furious, enraged, excited, wrathful, indignant, exasperated, aroused, inflamed

Answer—reply, respond, retort, acknowledge

Ask—question, inquire of, seek information from, put a question to, demand, request, expect, inquire, query, interrogate, examine, quiz

Awful—dreadful, terrible, abominable, bad, poor, unpleasant

Bad—evil, immoral, wicked, corrupt, sinful, depraved, rotten, contaminated, spoiled, tainted, harmful, injurious, unfavorable, defective, inferior, imperfect, substandard, faulty, improper, inappropriate, unsuitable, disagreeable, unpleasant, cross, nasty, unfriendly, irascible, horrible, atrocious, outrageous, scandalous, infamous, wrong, noxious, sinister, putrid, snide, deplorable, dismal, gross, heinous, nefarious, base, obnoxious, detestable, despicable, contemptible, foul, rank, ghastly, execrable

Beautiful—pretty, lovely, handsome, attractive, gorgeous, dazzling, splendid, magnificent, comely, fair, ravishing, graceful, elegant, fine, exquisite, aesthetic, pleasing, shapely, delicate, stunning, glorious, heavenly, resplendent, radiant, glowing, blooming, sparkling

Begin—start, open, launch, initiate, commence, inaugurate, originate

Big—enormous, huge, immense, gigantic, vast, colossal, gargantuan, large, sizeable, grand, great, tall, substantial, mammoth, astronomical, ample, broad, expansive, spacious, stout, tremendous, titanic, mountainous

Brave—courageous, fearless, dauntless, intrepid, plucky, daring, heroic, valorous, audacious, bold, gallant, valiant, doughty, mettlesome, plucky

Break—fracture, rupture, shatter, smash, wreck, crash, demolish, atomize

Bright—shining, shiny, gleaming, brilliant, sparkling, shimmering, radiant, vivid, colorful, lustrous, luminous, incandescent, intelligent, brilliant, knowing, quick-witted, smart, intellectual

Calm—quiet, peaceful, still, tranquil, mild, serene, smooth, composed, collected, unruffled, level-headed, unexcited, detached, aloof

Come—approach, advance, near, arrive, reach

Cool—chilly, cold, frosty, wintry, icy, frigid

Crooked—bent, twisted, curved, hooked, zigzag

Cry—shout, yell, yowl, scream, roar, bellow, weep, wail, sob, bawl

Cut—gash, slash, prick, nick, sever, slice, carve, cleave, slit, chop, crop, lop, reduce

Dangerous—perilous, hazardous, risky, uncertain, unsafe

Dark—shadowy, unlit, murky, gloomy, dim, dusky, shaded, sunless, black, dismal, sad, gloomy

Decide—determine, settle, choose, resolve

Definite—certain, sure, positive, determined, clear, distinct, obvious

Delicious—savory, delectable, appetizing, luscious, scrumptious, palatable, delightful, enjoyable, toothsome, exquisite

Describe—portray, characterize, picture, narrate, relate, recount, represent, report, record

Destroy—ruin, demolish, raze, waste, kill, slay, end, extinguish

Difference—disagreement, inequality, contrast, dissimilarity, incompatibility

Do—execute, enact, carry out, finish, conclude, effect, accomplish, achieve, attain

Dull—boring, tiring, tiresome, uninteresting, slow, dumb, stupid, unimaginative, lifeless, dead, insensible, tedious, wearisome, listless, expressionless, plain, monotonous, humdrum, dreary

Eager—keen, fervent, enthusiastic, involved, interested, alive to

End—stop, finish, terminate, conclude, close, halt, cessation, discontinuance

Enjoy—appreciate, delight in, be pleased, indulge in, luxuriate in, bask in, relish, devour, savor, like

Explain—elaborate, clarify, define, interpret, justify, account for

Fair—just, impartial, unbiased, objective, unprejudiced, honest

Fall—drop, descend, plunge, topple, tumble

False—fake, fraudulent, counterfeit, spurious, untrue, unfounded, erroneous, deceptive, groundless, fallacious

Famous—well-known, renowned, celebrated, famed, eminent, illustrious, distinguished, noted, notorious

Fast—quick, rapid, swift, speedy, fleet, hasty, snappy, mercurial, swiftly, rapidly, quickly, snappily, speedily, lickety-split, posthaste, hastily, expeditiously, like a flash

Fat—stout, corpulent, fleshy, beefy, paunchy, plump, full, rotund, tubby, pudgy, chubby, chunky, burly, bulky, hippopotamic, elphantine

Fear—fright, dread, terror, alarm, dismay, anxiety, scare, awe, horror, panic, apprehension

Fly—soar, hover, flit, wing, flee, waft, glide, coast, skim, sail, cruise

Funny—humorous, amusing, droll, comic, comical, laughable, silly

Get—acquire, obtain, secure, procure, gain, fetch, find, score, accumulate, win, earn, reap, catch, net, bag, derive, collect, gather, glean, pick up, accept, come by, regain, salvage

Go—recede, depart, fade, disappear, move, travel, proceed

Good—excellent, fine, superior, wonderful, marvelous, qualified, suited, suitable, apt, proper, capable, generous, kindly, friendly, gracious, obliging, pleasant, agreeable, pleasurable, satisfactory, well-behaved, obedient, honorable, reliable, trustworthy, safe, favorable, profitable, advantageous, righteous, expedient, helpful, valid, genuine, ample, salubrious, estimable, beneficial, splendid, great, noble, worthy, first-rate, top-notch, grand, sterling, superb, respectable, edifying

Great—noteworthy, worthy, distinguished, remarkable, grand, considerable, powerful, much, mighty

Gross—improper, rude, coarse, indecent, crude, vulgar, outrageous, extreme, grievous, shameful, uncouth, obscene, low

Happy—pleased, contented, satisfied, delighted, elated, joyful, cheerful, ecstatic, jubilant, gay, tickled, gratified, glad, blissful, overjoyed

Hate—depise, loathe, detest, abhor, disfavor, dislike, disapprove, abominate

Have—hold, possess, own, contain, acquire, gain, maintain, believe, bear, beget, occupy, absorb, fill, enjoy

Help—aid, assist, support, encourage, back, wait on, attend, serve, relieve, succor, benefit, befriend, abet

Hide—conceal, cover, mask, cloak, camouflage, screen, shroud, veil

Hurry—rush, run, speed, race, hasten, urge, accelerate, bustle

Hurt—damage, harm, injure, wound, distress, afflict, pain

Idea—thought, concept, conception, notion, understanding, opinion, plan, view, belief

Important—necessary, vital, critical, indispensable, valuable, essential, significant, primary, principal, considerable, famous, distinguished, notable, well-known

Interesting—fascinating, engaging, sharp, keen, bright, intelligent, animated, spirited, attractive, inviting, intriguing, provocative, thought-provoking, challenging, inspiring, involving, moving, titillating, tantalizing, exciting, entertaining, piquant, lively, racy, spicy, engrossing, absorbing, consuming, gripping, arresting, enthralling, spellbinding, curious, captivating, enchanting, bewitching, appealing,

Keep—hold, retain, withhold, preserve, maintain, sustain, support

Kill—slay, execute, assassinate, murder, destroy, cancel, abolish

Lazy—indolent, slothful, idle, inactive, sluggish

Little—tiny, small, diminutive, shrimp, runt, miniature, puny, exiguous, dinky, cramped, limited, itsy-bitsy, microscopic, slight, petite, minute

Look—gaze, see, glance, watch, survey, study, seek, search for, peek, peep, glimpse, stare, contemplate, examine, gape, ogle, scrutinize, inspect, leer, behold, observe, view, witness, perceive, spy, sight, discover, notice, recognize, peer, eye, gawk, peruse, explore

Love—like, admire, esteem, fancy, care for, cherish, adore, treasure, worship, appreciate, savor

Make—create, originate, invent, beget, form, construct, design, fabricate, manufacture, produce, build, develop, do, effect, execute, compose, perform, accomplish, earn, gain, obtain, acquire, get

Mark—label, tag, price, ticket, impress, effect, trace, imprint, stamp, brand, sign, note, heed, notice, designate

Mischievous—prankish, playful, naughty, roguish, waggish, impish, sportive

Move—plod, go, creep, crawl, inch, poke, drag, toddle, shuffle, trot, dawdle, walk, traipse, mosey, jog, plug, trudge, stump, lumber, trail, lag, run, sprint, trip, bound, hotfoot, high-tail, streak, stride, tear, breeze, whisk, rush, dash, dart, bolt, fling, scamper, scurry, skedaddle, scoot, scuttle, scramble, race, chase, hasten, hurry, hump, gallop, lope, accelerate, stir, budge, travel, wander, roam, journey, trek, ride, spin, slip, glide, slide, slither, coast, flow, sail, saunter, hobble, amble, stagger, paddle, slouch, prance, straggle, meander, perambulate, waddle, wobble, pace, swagger, promenade, lunge

Moody—temperamental, changeable, short-tempered, glum, morose, sullen, mopish, irritable, testy, peevish, fretful, spiteful, sulky, touchy

Neat—clean, orderly, tidy, trim, dapper, natty, smart, elegant, well-organized, super, desirable, spruce, shipshape, well-kept, shapely

New—fresh, unique, original, unusual, novel, modern, current, recent

Old—feeble, frail, ancient, weak, aged, used, worn, dilapidated, ragged, faded, broken-down, former, old-fashioned, outmoded, passe, veteran, mature, venerable, primitive, traditional, archaic, conventional, customary, stale, musty, obsolete, extinct

Part—portion, share, piece, allotment, section, fraction, fragment

Place—space, area, spot, plot, region, location, situation, position, residence, dwelling, set, site, station, status, state

Plan—plot, scheme, design, draw, map, diagram, procedure, arrangement, intention, device, contrivance, method, way, blueprint

Popular—well-liked, approved, accepted, favorite, celebrated, common, current

Predicament—quandary, dilemma, pickle, problem, plight, spot, scrape, jam

Put—place, set, attach, establish, assign, keep, save, set aside, effect, achieve, do, build

Quiet—silent, still, soundless, mute, tranquil, peaceful, calm, restful

Right—correct, accurate, factual, true, good, just, honest, upright, lawful, moral, proper, suitable, apt, legal, fair

Run—race, speed, hurry, hasten, sprint, dash, rush, escape, elope, flee

Say/Tell—inform, notify, advise, relate, recount, narrate, explain, reveal, disclose, divulge, declare, command, order, bid, enlighten, instruct, insist, teach, train, direct, issue, remark, converse, speak, affirm, suppose, utter, negate, express, verbalize, voice, articulate, pronounce, deliver, convey, impart, assert, state, allege, mutter, mumble, whisper, sigh, exclaim, yell, sing, yelp, snarl, hiss, grunt, snort, roar, bellow, thunder, boom, scream, shriek, screech, squawk, whine, philosophize, stammer, stutter, lisp, drawl, jabber, protest, announce, swear, vow, contend, assure, deny dispute

Scared—afraid, frightened, alarmed, terrified, panicked, fearful, unnerved, insecure, timid, shy, skittish, jumpy, disquieted, worried, vexed, troubled, disturbed, horrified, terrorized, shocked, petrified, haunted, timorous, shrinking, tremulous, stupefied, paralyzed, stunned, apprehensive

Show—display, exhibit, present, note, point to, indicate, explain, reveal, prove, demonstrate, expose

Slow—unhurried, gradual, leisurely, late, behind, tedious, slack

Stop—cease, halt, stay, pause, discontinue, conclude, end, finish, quit

Story—tale, myth, legend, fable, yarn, account, narrative, chronicle, epic, sage, anecdote, record, memoir

Strange—odd, peculiar, unusual, unfamiliar, uncommon, queer, wierd, outlandish, curious, unique, exclusive, irregular

Take—hold, catch, seize, grasp, win, capture, acquire, pick, choose, select, prefer, remove, steal, lift, rob, engage, bewitch, purchase, buy, retract, recall, assume, occupy, consume

Tell—disclose, reveal, show, expose, uncover, relate, narrate, inform, advise, explain, divulge, declare, command, order, bid, recount, repeat

Think—judge, deem, assume, believe, consider, contemplate, reflect, meditate

Trouble—distress, anguish, anxiety, worry, wretchedness, pain, danger, peril, disaster, grief, misfortune, difficulty, concern, pains, inconvenience, exertion, effort

True—accurate, right, proper, precise, exact, valid, genuine, real, actual, trusty, steady, loyal, dependable, sincere, staunch

Ugly—hideous, frightful, frightening, shocking, horrible, unpleasant, monstrous, terrifying, gross, grisly, ghastly, horrid, unsightly, plain, homely, evil, repulsive, repugnant, gruesome

Unhappy—miserable, uncomfortable, wretched, heart-broken, unfortunate, poor, downhearted, sorrowful, depressed, dejected, melancholy, glum, gloomy, dismal, discouraged, sad

Use—employ, utilize, exhaust, spend, expend, consume, exercise

Wrong—incorrect, inaccurate, mistaken, erroneous, improper, unsuitable

wish	dream	boy	girl	match	love	miss
dish	cream	ahoy	curl	batch	above	bliss
fish	gleam	coy	hurl	catch	dove	hiss
squish	seam	enjoy	pearl	hatch	glove	kiss
swish	team	joy	swirl	latch	of	sis
	steam	toy	twirl	patch	shove	this

cat	bunk	ball	weak	think	rain
bat	clunk	call	beak	blink	cane
fat	dunk	crawl	cheek	brink	gain
flat	drunk	fall	leak	clink	lain
hat	hunk	gall	meek	drink	main
mat	junk	hall	peak	link	pain
pat	punk	mall	peek	pink	rain
rat	sunk	stall	reek	rink	stain
sat	stunk	tall	seek	sink	train
slat	trunk	wall	week	wink	vain

and	bare	black	block	blue	date
band	bear	back	clock	clue	ate
brand	care	crack	cock	crew	bait
canned	dare	lack	dock	drew	fate
fanned	fare	pack	flock	few	gate
gland	hair	quack	knock	flew	hate
grand	pear	rack	lock	glue	late
hand	rare	sack	mock	knew	mate
land	stare	smack	rock	new	rate
sand	there	stack	sock	to	state
stand	wear	track	tock	true	wait

day	dear	eye	four	friend	gold
clay	deer	by	core	bend	bold
gay	fear	cry	door	blend	bowled
hay	hear	fry	floor	end	cold
lay	here	I	more	lend	fold
may	near	high	pour	mend	hold
play	peer	lie	roar	pretend	mold
ray	queer	pie	sore	rend	old
say	rear	sigh	store	send	rolled
tray	steer	tie	tore	spend	sold
way	year	why	wore	tend	told

17

book	burn	time	fist	five	six	ten
brook	churn	crime	grist	chive	fix	been
cook	earn	dime	hissed	dive	kicks	den
crook	fern	grime	kissed	drive	licks	hen
hook	learn	lime	list	hive	picks	men
look	stern	rhyme	mist	jive	sticks	pen
rook	turn	slime	twist	live	ticks	when
took	yearn				wicks	yen

dog	thought	star	tin	bowl	man
cog	bought	are	bin	coal	ban
fog	brought	bar	din	foal	can
flog	caught	car	fin	goal	fan
frog	fought	far	gin	hole	pan
hog	ought	jar	kin	mole	plan
jog	sought	mar	pin	pole	ran
log	taught	tar	sin	roll	tan
smog	taut	war	win	soul	van

grade	green	map	night	nine	ring
ade	bean	cap	bite	dine	bring
blade	clean	clap	bright	fine	cling
fade	dean	flap	fight	line	ding
glade	glean	gap	kite	mine	fling
laid	keen	lap	light	pine	king
made	lean	nap	quite	sign	sing
maid	mean	slap	right	swine	sling
paid	queen	tap	sight	tine	sting
raid	seen	trap	tight	vine	swing
wade	teen	wrap	white	whine	wing

room	run	tale	three	tone	snow
boom	bun	dale	be	bone	blow
bloom	done	fail	flea	cone	crow
broom	fun	gale	glee	groan	flow
doom	gun	hale	key	known	go
gloom	none	jail	knee	lone	know
groom	one	male	me	moan	low
loom	pun	nail	see	phone	mow
room	sun	pale	tea	stone	no
tomb	ton	rail	tree	thrown	row
zoom	won	sale	we	zone	so

A **period** is used:
1. At the end of a declarative sentence.
2. At the end of an imperative sentence.
3. After numerals and letters in outlines.
4. At the end of a business request stated in question form.
5. After an abbreviation or an initial.

A **question mark** is used:
1. At the end of an interrogative sentence.
2. Inside parentheses after a date or statement to show doubt.

An **exclamation point** is used:
1. At the end of an exclamatory sentence.
2. After a very strong interjection.
3. At the end of an imperative sentence that exclaims.

A **comma** is used:
1. To separate items in a series.
2. To separate adjectives of equal value.
3. To separate a direct quotation from the rest of a sentence.
4. To separate the day of the month from the year.
5. To separate the names of a city and a state.
6. To separate a name from a title (David Bird, President)
7. To set off adjectives in an appositive position.
8. To set off introductory words like *no* and *now.*
9. To set off words like *however, moreover, too.*
10. To set off a name used in direct address.
11. To set off a nonrestrictive adjective clause.
12. To set off most words used in apposition.
13. After the greeting in a friendly letter.
14. After the closing in any letter.
15. After a last name preceding a first name.
16. After a mild interjection within a sentence.
17. After an introductory adverbial clause.
18. After an introductory participial phrase.
19. Before the conjunction in a compound sentence.
20. Whenever necessary to make meaning clear.

An **apostrophe** is used:
1. To show possession.
2. In contractions.
3. To form plurals of letters, figures, signs, and words.

Quotation marks are used:
1. To enclose the exact words of a speaker.
2. Around titles of short plays, short stories, short poems, chapter titles, and songs.

A **colon** is used:
1. In writing time (6:45).
2. To introduce a list.
3. After the greeting in a business letter.
4. In written plays and in other forms of written dialogue, after the name of the character who is speaking.

A **semicolon** is used:
1. To join independent clauses in a compound sentence when a conjuntion is not present.
2. To precede a conjunctive adverb (therefore, however, furthermore, etc.) used between the coordinate clauses of a compound sentence.
3. In place of a comma when a more distinct pause than a comma indicates is desired.

Underlining is used:
1. Below handwritten or typewritten titles of movies, newspapers, books, magazines, ships, and trains.
2. To set off foreign words and phrases which are not yet part of the English language.

A **hyphen** is used:
1. In writing compound numbers.
2. To divide a word at the end of a line.
3. Between parts of a compound adjective preceding a noun.

A **dash** is used:
1. To indicate an abrubt break in thought or structure.
2. To indicate a parenthetical or explanatory phrase or clause.
3. Between numbers in a page reference.

Parentheses are used:
1. To enclose material that is supplementary, explanatory, or interpretive.
2. To enclose a question mark after a date or a statement to show doubt.
3. To enclose an author's insertion or comment.

Capitalize the first letter in:

1. The first word of a sentence.
2. The first word in each line of poetry.
3. The first and all other important words in the greeting of a letter.
4. The first word in the closing of a letter.
5. The first, last, and other main words in titles of chapters, stories, poems, reports, songs, books, movies, and radio and television programs.
6. The word I.
7. A proper adjective.
8. Initials.
9. Titles of persons (Mr., Ms., Mrs., Dr.).
10. Abbreviations (P.O., R.R., C.O.D., Dr.).
11. Titles of high government officials.
12. A proper noun.
13. Words like Mother, Sister, Uncle when used in place of or with names.
14. Names of schools, clubs, organizations, and buildings.
15. Names of streets, avenues, boulevards, roads, and Rural Route.
16. Names of cities, towns, counties, states, countries, and continents.
17. Names of rivers, oceans, mountains, and regions (the South).
18. Names of days, months, holidays, and other special days.
19. Names of businesses and special products.
20. Names of languages, nationalities, and special groups.
21. Names of political parties.
22. Names of government departments.
23. Names for the Deity.
24. Names of churches and religious denominations.
25. Names of historical events and documents.
26. Names of airlines, ships, and railroads.
27. Names of magazines and newspapers.
28. The first word of a head and a subhead in outlines.
29. The first word after a strong interjection.

BLOCK STYLE

(your street address)   *
(your city, state, and Zip)   *   Heading
(the date)

(addressee's name)
(company's name)   Inside Address
(company's street address)
(company's city, state, and Zip)

_____ :   Greeting/Salutation

_____
_____
_____
_____   Body of Letter
_____
_____

_____
_____

_____ .   Complimentary Close

(your handwritten name)   Signature
(your typed name)

* Do not include if you are using paper with a letterhead on it.

MODIFIED BLOCK

Heading

                    (your street address)   *
                    (your city, state, and Zip) *
                    (the date)

(addressee's name)
(company's name)   Inside Address
(company's street address)
(company's city, state, and Zip)

_____ :   Greeting/Salutation

_____
_____
_____
_____   Body of Letter
_____
_____
_____

Complimentary Close   _____

Signature   (your handwritten name)
                                 (your typed name)

* Do not include if you are using paper with a letterhead on it.

MODIFIED SEMIBLOCK

Heading

                    (your street address)   *
                    (your city, state, and Zip) *
                    (the date)

(addressee's name)
(company's name)   Inside Address
(company's street address)
(company's city, state, and Zip)

_____ :   Greeting/Salutation

_____
_____
_____

_____
_____   Body of Letter
_____
_____
_____
_____

Complimentary Close   _____

Signature   (your handwritten name)
                                 (your typed name)

* Do not include if you are using paper with a letterhead on it.

FRIENDLY LETTER

Heading

                    (your street address)   *
                    (your city, state, and Zip) *
                    (the date)

_____ ,   Greeting/Salutation

_____
_____
_____
_____   **Body of Letter**
_____
_____
_____
_____
_____
_____
_____
_____

Complimentary Close   _____

Signature   _____

* Do not include if this information is printed or engraved on your stationery.

HANDWRITING SAMPLER

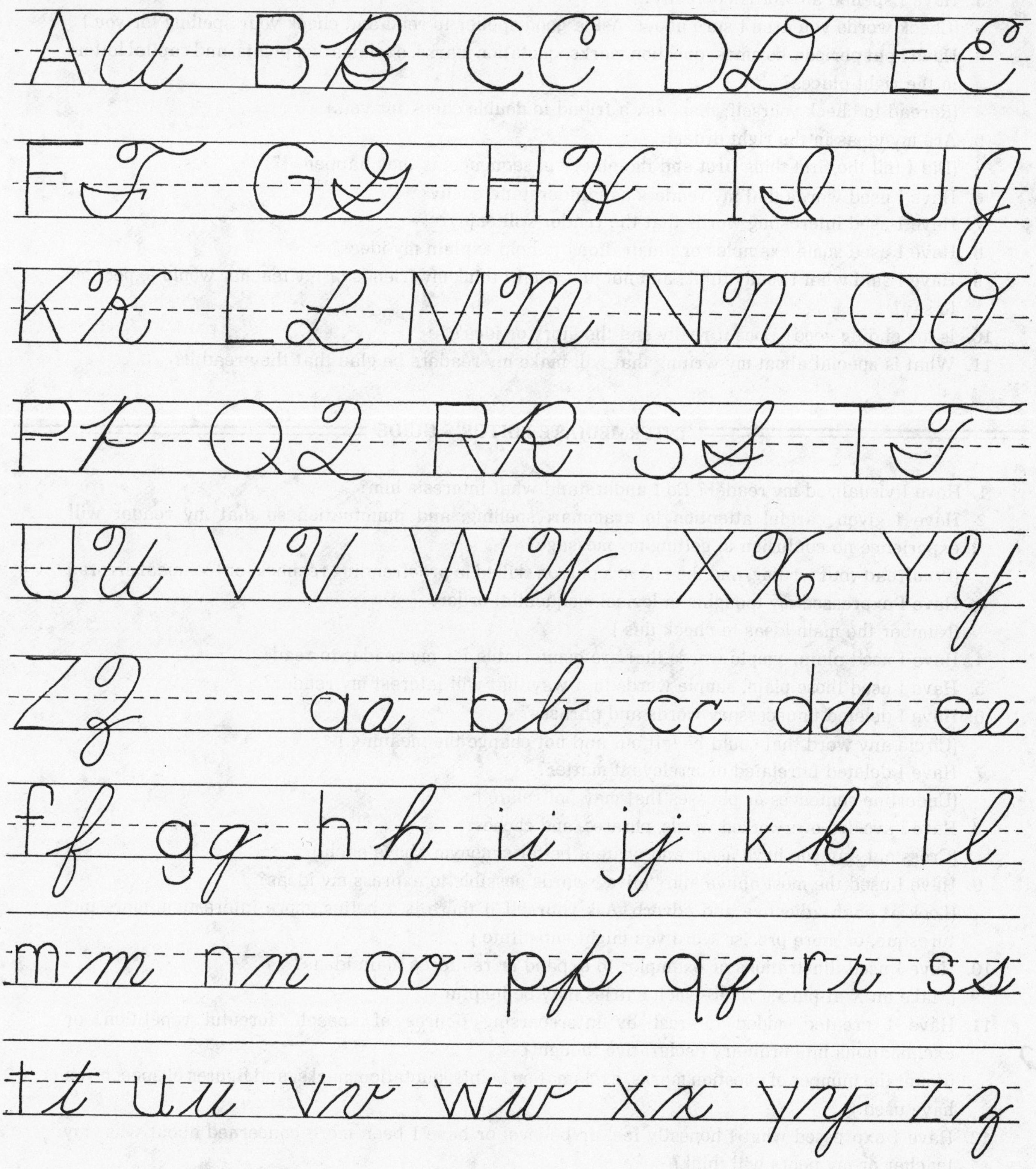
A a B b C c D d E e
F f G g H h I i J j
K k L l M m N n O o
P p Q q R r S s T t
U u V v W w X x Y y
Z z a a b b c c d d e e
f f g g h h i i j j k k l l
m m n n o o p p q q r r s s
t t u u v v w w x x y y z z

1. Who will read my work?
2. Will they find it interesting?
3. Have I spelled all words correctly?
   (Check words you aren't sure about. Ask a good speller to read and check your spelling for you.)
4. Have I put periods, commas, question marks, quotation marks, exclamation points, and capital letters in the right places?
   (Reread to check yourself; then, ask a friend to double-check for you.)
5. Are my ideas in the right order?
   (Did I tell the first thing first and the others in sequence as they happened?)
6. Have I used words that my readers can understand easily?
7. Have I used interesting words that the reader will enjoy?
8. Have I used some examples or illustrations to help explain my ideas?
9. Have I said what I really think, and not just what I think my friends or my teacher would expect me to say?
10. Is my ending good? Does it really end the story or idea?
11. What is special about my writing that will make my readers be glad that they read it?

1. Have I visualized my reader? Do I understand what interests him?
2. Have I given careful attention to grammar, spelling, and punctuation so that my reader will experience no confusion in getting my message?
   (Proofread your writing, and then have a person skilled in proofreading recheck for technical errors.)
3. Have I expressed my thoughts in logical, sequential order?
   (Number the main ideas to check this.)
4. Have I used plain, simple words that are comfortable for my reader to read?
5. Have I used those plain, simple words in a way that will interest my reader?
6. Have I deleted unnecessary words and phrases?
   (Circle any word that could be left out and not change the meaning.)
7. Have I deleted unrelated or irrelevant matter?
   (Underline sentences or phrases that may not relate.)
8. Have I avoided overworked words, phrases, and clichés?
   (Cross out any you have used, and write a better synonym above each.)
9. Have I used the most active and "alive" words possible to express my ideas?
   (Look at each adjective and adverb. Ask yourself if there is a better, more interesting, more picturesque, or more precise word you might substitute.)
10. Have I used illustrations or examples to expand or reinforce main ideas?
    (Make an X at places where such entries may be helpful.)
11. Have I created added interest by interspersing figures of speech, forceful repetition, or exclamations into ordinary declarative thought?
    (Count the number of question marks, exclamation points, quotation marks, and figures of speech you have used.)
12. Have I expressed what I honestly feel or believe, or have I been more concerned about what my teacher or my peers will think?
    (Use tact and sensitivity in expressing negative or unpopular feelings or ideas, but do not sacrifice clarity or effectiveness.)
13. Have I referred to the beginning in the ending, and left my reader with an idea to ponder?
    (Will the reader feel that the article has been concluded thoughtfully? Have you said anything that will cause him to reconsider the subject?)

Instruction	Mark in Margin	Mark in Type	Corrected Type
Delete	*(delete symbol)*	the ~~good~~ word	the word
Insert indicated material	good	the word	the good word
Let it stand	stet	the ~~good~~ word	the good word
Make capital	cap	the word	the Word
Make lower case	lc	The Word	the Word
Set in small capitals	sc	See word.	See WORD.
Set in italic type	ital	The word is word.	The word is *word*.
Set in roman type	rom	the *word*	the word
Set in boldface type	bf	the entry word	the entry **word**
Set in lightface type	lf	the entry **word**	the entry word
Transpose	tr	the word good	the good word
Close up space	*(close up symbol)*	the wo rd	the word
Delete and close up space	*(symbol)*	the woord	the word
Spell out	sp	②words	two words
Insert: space	#	theword	the word
period	⊙	This is the word	This is the word.
comma	⌃	words words, words	words, words, words
hyphen	=	word for word test	word-for-word test
colon	⊙	The following words	The following words:
semicolon	⌃	Scan the words skim the words.	Scan the words; skim the words.
apostrophe	⌄	Johns words	John's words
quotation marks	⌄/⌄	the word word	the word "word"
parentheses	(/)/	The word word is in parentheses.	The word (word) is in parentheses.
brackets	[/]/	He read from the Word the Bible.	He read from the Word [the Bible].
en dash	1/N	1964 1972	1964–1972
em dash	1/M /1/M/	The dictionary how often it is needed belongs in every home.	The dictionary—how often it is needed—belongs in every home.
superior type	⌄	$2 = 4$	$2^2 = 4$
inferior type	⌃	HO	H_2O
asterisk	⌄	word	word*
dagger	†	a word	a word†
double dagger	‡	words and words	words and words‡
section symbol	§	Book Reviews	§Book Reviews
virgule	/	either or	either/or
Start paragraph	¶	"Where is it?" "It's on the shelf."	"Where is it?" "It's on the shelf."
Run in	run in	The entry word is printed in boldface. The pronunciation follows.	The entry word is printed in boldface. The pronunciation follows.
Turn right side up	↻	the word	the word
Move left	⊏	⊏ the word	the word
Move right	⊐	the word	the word
Move up	⊓	the word	the word
Move down	⊔	the word	the word
Align	‖	the word the word the word	the word the word the word
Straighten line	=	the word	the word
Wrong font	wf	the word	the word
Broken type	✕	the word	the word

Abstract Noun—a noun that names things which do not have a physical substance.
Example: *compassion.*

Active Voice—a verb which expresses action and can take a direct object.
Example: I *threw* the ball.

Adjective—a word that modifies a noun or a pronoun.
Example: the *white* ball.

Adverb—a word that modifies a verb, an adjective, or another adverb.
Example: Go *slowly.*

Antecendent—the word, phrase, or clause to which a relative pronoun refers. A pronoun must agree with its antecendent in number.
Example: *Erin* gave me his ball.

Articles—the adjectives *a*, *an*, and *the.*

Auxiliary Verb—a verb that accompanies another verb to show tense, mood, or voice.
Example: She *has* gone.

Clause—a group of words that contains a subject and a predicate, and forms part of a compound or complex sentence.
Example: *After I left, she called.*

Collective Noun—a noun that denotes a collection of persons or things regarded as a unit; usually takes a singular verb.
Example: The *committee* chooses its own chairman.

Common Noun—a noun that indicates any one of a class of persons, places, or things.
Examples: *boy; town; ball.*

Comparative Adjective—an adjective form (ending in —er or adding the word *more* before the word) used when two person or things are compared.
Example: This apple is *smaller* and *more delicious* than that one.

Complex Sentence—a sentence containing one independent clause and one or more dependent clauses.
Example: *I went to town to shop, but found that all the stores were closed.*

Compound Sentence—a sentence containing two or more independent clauses joined by a conjunction.
Example: *I called my friend, and we talked for an hour.*

Compound-Complex Sentence—a sentence that has two or more independent clauses and at least one dependent or subordinate clause.
Example: *When she opened the door, there was no one on the porch, and the street was empty, too.*

Concrete Noun—a noun that names a physical, visible, or tangible item.
Example: *airplane.*

Conjunction—a word that connects words, phrases, or clauses.
Example: I like toast *and* jam.

Coordinating Conjunction—a conjunction used to connect two independent clauses.
Example: He grinned, *and* I giggled.

Correlative Conjuction—conjunctions which are used in pairs.
Example: *Neither* Alan *nor* Amy will go.

Dependent (or Subordinate) Clause— a clause that functions as a noun, adjective, or adverb within a sentence, but cannot stand alone.
Example: *What she said* was true.

Direct Object— the noun, pronoun, or noun phrase in a sentence which receives the action of a transitive verb.
Example: I threw the *ball.*

Gerund— a verb form ending in *-ing,* usually used as a noun.
Example: *Skiing* is fun.

Indefinite Pronoun— a pronoun that does not specify the identity of its object.
Example: *Anyone* can come.

Independent Clause— a clause which contains at least a subject and a predicate, and is capable of standing alone.
Example: *I went to the store.*

Indirect Object— the noun, pronoun, or noun phrase named as the one to or for whom action involving a direct object is done.
Example: He threw *me* the ball.

Infinitive— a non-inflected verb form usually preceeded by *to,* used as a noun, adjective, or adverb.
Example: *To run* fast is fun.

Intensive Pronoun— a pronoun which is used for emphasis.
Example: I *myself* saw it.

Interjection— an exclamatory word or phrase.
Example: *Hey! Look out!*

Intransitive Verb— a verb that cannot take an object.
Example: She *learns* easily.

Linking Verb— a verb that can be followed by an adjective that modifies the subject.
Example: Randy *is* tall.

Modify— to qualify or limit the meaning of.
Example: *very* small.

Noun— a word that names a person, place, or thing.
Examples: *girl; city; hat.*

Paragraph— a distinct division within a written work that may consist of several sentences or just one, that expresses something relevant to the whole work but is complete within itself.

Passive Voice— a verb which expresses state of being and cannot take a direct object.
Example: He *was asked* to leave.

Past Tense— a verb form that expresses action or condition that occurred in the past.
Example: Yesterday I *went* to town.

Personal Pronoun— a pronoun that denotes the speaker, person spoken to, or person spoken about.
Example: *You* can find it.

Positive Adjective— an adjective form used to assign a quality to the word it modifies.
Example: the *fast* car.

Possessive Pronoun— a pronoun that shows possession.
Example: That car is *mine.*

Predicate— the portion of a sentence or clause that tells something about the subject, consisting of a verb and possibly including objects, modifiers, and/or verb complements.

Predicate Adjective—an adjective that refers to, describes, or limits the subject of a sentence.
Example: The rock is *heavy*.

Predicate Nominative—a noun following a form of the verb *to be* in a sentence which modifies the subject.
Example: She is *Alicia*.

Preposition—a word that shows relationship (often between verbs and nouns or nouns and nouns) and takes an object.
Example: Put it *on* the table.

Prepositional Phrase—a group of words in a sentence that includes a preposition and its object, along with any modifiers of the object.
Example: Put it *on the first table*.

Present Tense—a verb form that expresses current time.
Example: I *am* here.

Pronoun—a word that takes the place of a noun.
Example: *I; you; she; it; he*.

Proper Noun—a noun that names a particular person, place, or thing, and is capitalized.
Examples: *Omaha; Jenny*.

Reflexive Pronoun—a pronoun that ends in -self or -selves; used to point the action back to the subject.
Example: You will hurt *yourself*.

Relative Pronoun—a pronoun that shows a relationship.
Example: It was he *who* did it.

Run-On (or Fused) Sentence—a sentence in which two complete sentences are run together with no punctuation to separate them.
Example: *I went to the movie I ate some popcorn*.

Sentence—a basic unit of language which must contain a subject and a predicate.
Example: *I went to the movie*.

Subject—a word or phrase in a sentence that is the doer of the action, or receives the action (in passive voice), or which is described; must agree in number with the predicate.
Example: *Margaret* was there.

Subjunctive (or Conditional) Mood—a set of verb forms used to express contingent or hypothetical action, usually introduced by *if, that,* etc., and always taking the plural form of the verb.
Example: *If I were you*, I'd go.

Superlative Adjective—an adjective form (ending in —*est* or adding the word *most* before the word) used when three or more things are involved in a comparison.
Example: This is the *slowest* of all cars.

Transitive—a verb which can take an object within a sentence.
Example: He *threw* the ball.

Verb—a word that shows action, state of being, or occurrence.
Examples: *run; is; find*.

Author	Selected Works	Writing Style Specialty
Alcott, Louisa May	*Little Women* *Little Men*	Characterization
Andersen, Hans Christian	*Andersen's Fairy Tales*	Fantasy
Blume, Judith	*Are You There, God? It's Me, Margaret.* *Then Again, Maybe I Won't*	Plot and Sequence
Carroll, Lewis	*Alice's Adventures in Wonderland* *Through the Looking Glass*	Imagery
Cather, Willa	*My Antonia* *Death Comes for the Archbishop*	Characterization; Plot and Sequence
cummings, e. e.	*Tulips and Chimneys* *Poems 1923-1954*	Poetry
Dahl, Roald	*Charlie and the Chocolate Factory* *The Magic Finger*	Plot and Sequence
Dickens, Charles	*A Christmas Carol* *David Copperfield*	Simple ideas, beautifully expressed
Grimm, Jacob and Wilhelm	*Grimms' Fairy Tales*	Fantasy
Halliburton, Richard	*The Royal Road to Romance* *The Flying Carpet*	Journalism
Henry, O.	*The Four Million* *Works of O. Henry*	Short Story Mastery
Keats, Ezra Jack	*The Snowy Day* *Whistle for Willie*	Simple ideas, beautifully expressed
Kipling, Rudyard	*The Jungle Books* *Just So Stories*	Plot and Sequence
Krauss, Ruth	*A Hole Is to Dig* *A Very Special House*	Simple ideas, beautifully expressed
Lear, Edward	*The Complete Nonsense Book* *The Jumblies*	Humor
L'Engle, Madeline	*A Wrinkle in Time* *Meet the Austins*	Plot and Sequence
Longfellow, Henry W.	*Voices of the Night* *Ballads and Other Poems*	Poetry
McCloskey, Robert	*Make Way for Ducklings* *Time of Wonder*	Plot and Sequence
Milne, A. A.	*When We Were Very Young* *Now We Are Six*	Rhythm

SELECTED AUTHORS YOUNG WRITERS SHOULD READ

Author	Selected Works	Writing Style Specialty
Nash, Ogden	*Good Intentions* *I'm a Stranger Here Myself*	Humor; Coined Words
Riley, James Whitcomb	*The Old Swimmin' Hole* *'Leven More Poems*	Poetry
Rossetti, Christina	*Sing Song* *Goblin Market and Other Poems*	Poetry
Sandburg, Carl	*Rootabaga Stories* *Wind Song*	Description; Figures of Speech
Sendak, Maurice	*Where the Wild Things Are* *In The Night Kitchen*	Fantasy
Seuss, Dr.	*The Cat in the Hat* *Bartholomew and the Oobleck*	Coined Words; Originality
Silverstein, Shel	*Where the Sidewalk Ends* *Lafcadio*	Divergent Thinking; Humor
Steele, William O.	*The Perilous Road* *Wayah of the Real People*	Plot and Sequence
Stevenson, Robert Louis	*A Child's Garden of Verses*	Poetry
Teasdale, Sara	*Stars Tonight* *Strange Victory*	Lovely Word Usage
Tolkien, J. R. R.	*The Hobbit* *Lord of the Rings*	Creating a believable mythical world
Twain, Mark	*The Adventures of Tom Sawyer* *The Adventures of Huckleberry Finn*	Characterization; Description
Viorst, Judith	*Alexander and the Terrible, Horrible, No Good, Very Bad Day* *Alexander, Who Use to Be Rich Last Sunday*	Brings extraordinary qualities to everyday experiences
White, E. B.	*Charlotte's Web* *The Trumpet of the Swan*	Description; Imagery
Zoloto, Charlotte	*A Father Like That* *When I Have a Son*	Simple ideas, beautifully expressed

Dictionaries

The American Heritage Dictionary of the English Language
W. Morris, ed. American Heritage Pub. Co./Houghton Mifflin
Bernstein's Reverse Dictionary
Bernstein. The New York Times Book Co.
The Complete Rhyming Dictionary
C. Wood, ed. Doubleday & Co.
Doublespeak Dictionary
W. Lambdin. Pinnacle.
Macmillan Dictionary for Children
P. R. Winant, sup. ed. Macmillan Pub. Co., Inc.
New Rhyming Dictionary and Poet's Handbook
Hohnson. Harper & Row.
Webster's New World Speller/Divider
_____. W. Collins, Pub.
Webster's Seventh New Collegiate Dictionary
_____. G. and C. Merriam Co.

Grammar and Usage

The Art of Styling Sentences
Waddell, Esch, and Walker. Barrons.
The Complete Letter Writer
N. H. and S. K. Mager. Simon & Schuster.
The Golden Book on Writing
Lambuth. Penguin.
Instant Vocabulary
Ehrlich. Pocket Books.
Letters for All Occasions
Myers. Barnes and Noble.
The New York Times Manual of Style and Usage
L. Jordan, ed. Quadrangle/The New York Times Book Co.
Use the Right Word
S. I. Hayakawa, ed. The Reader's Digest Assn., Inc.
Word Watcher's Handbook
Martin. David McKay Co., Inc.
Write It Right
Kredenser. Barnes and Noble.
The Written Word
A. D. Steinhardt, sup. ed. Houghton Mifflin.

Quotations and Slang

Bartlett's Familiar Quotations
E. M. Beck, ed. Little, Brown & Co.
Dictionary of American Slang
Wentworth and Flexner. Simon and Schuster.
The International Thesaurus of Quotations
R. T. Tripp, comp. Thomas Y. Crowell Co.

Thesauri

A Basic Dictionary of Synonyms and Antonyms
L. Urdang. Elsevier/Nelson Books.
The Clear and Simple Thesaurus Dictionary
Wittels and Greisman. Grosset and Dunlap.
Roget's International Thesaurus, 3rd ed.
_____. Thomas Y. Crowell Co.
The Word Finder
E. J. Fluck, et al. Rodale Press.